God Loves the Arabs, Too

Louis Bahjat Hamada, Ph.D.

TO SOW THE FALLOW SOIL

Winston-Derek Publishers, Inc.
Pennywell Drive—Post Office Box 90883
Nashville, Tennessee 37209

First printing 1986

Second printing 1988

Scripture quotations are from the King James Version of the Bible.

Library of Congress Catalog-in-Publication Data

Hamada, Louis Bahjat.
    God loves the Arabs, too.

    Bibliography: p.
    1. Civilization, Arab—Miscellanea. 2. Jewish-Arab relations—Religious aspects—Miscellanea. 4. Christianity and other religions—Islam—Miscellanea. I. Title.
DS36.8.H36 1985   909'.0974927   85-40888
ISBN 1-555230-00-8

Printed in the United States of America

PUBLISHED BY WINSTON-DEREK PUBLISHERS, INC.
Nashville, Tennessee 37205

Contents

I dedicate this book to my dear Lord and Savior Jesus Christ, who lovingly bestowed upon me the needed amount of understanding, strength, comfort, and guidance to finish this study. Moreover, I acknowledge the fact that without the illuminating power of the blessed Holy Spirit, this book would never have been written. May God graciously use it to his glory; and may he bring many Arabs, Jews, and others to a saving knowledge of his beloved Son, Christ Jesus!

Louis Bahjat Hamada, Ph.D.
P. O. Box 3333
Jackson, TN 38303
(901) 668-8350

Dr. Hamada may be contacted for speaking engagements at the above address.

Introduction

For years, I have felt the Lord Jesus compelling me to write about the Arabs and the Jews. But for one reason or another, I have procrastinated. I have made all kinds of excuses, supported by logical reasoning. What can I say that has not been said before? If I question popular and established beliefs regarding Israel, what will happen to my young and struggling faith-ministry? Would I lose many friends and much financial support by questioning the widespread dogma that the Jews are still the "chosen people" of God? How can I write objectively without being accused of taking sides with my people, the Arabs? Because English is not my native language, would I be able to impart my thoughts in a clear and concise manner without sounding opinionated? And who would publish such a book? These are but a few of the plausible excuses that I allowed to keep me from undertaking such a unique and adventurous journey.

However, my unexpected recent missionary visit to Israel provided the impetus needed to begin this long-awaited work. After witnessing the dehumanization of Arabs in Israel, where Jews, the once oppressed, have become the oppressors, my heart was filled with grief, and anguish for the neglected Arabs gripped my soul.

It is not my intention to take sides in the centuries-old conflict between Arabs and Jews, but rather to explore the teachings of the Word of God. The aim of this study is to prayerfully delineate the inescapable fact "that God is no respecter of persons: But in every nation he that feareth him, and worketh righteousness, is accepted with him . . . preaching peace by Jesus Christ . . . that through his name whosoever believeth in him shall receive remission of sins" (Acts 10:34-43). More specifically, I will explore briefly the origin and heritage of Arabs and Jews as related to the eternal plan of God, calling into question several widely held myths concerning the biblical teachings about these two peoples. This will be done by demonstrating two facts as taught in the Bible. First, I will show that Jews, originally set apart by God as a people peculiar to himself, now act as his prophetic time clock. And second, I will show that Arabs not only are the descendants of Abraham through Hagar, the Egyptian maid, but more important, they are the children of Eber, a great-grandson of Shem, the son of Noah.

Very little systematic research has been done on the origin and heritage of the Arabs and the Jews as revealed in the Bible. The few studies that have been made are inadequate and leave many questions unanswered. Why do prejudices and feelings of racial superiority exist today between Arabs and Jews? Why are so many European and American Christians using their God-given abilities to provoke the Arabs to wrath by taking sides politically with Israel, while turning a deaf ear to the spiritual famine of the Arab world? Since the Bible teaches that God's love is universal, why do certain Western evangelists and Bible teachers fail to preach a balanced view of the gospel? Did not God send his Son to be the propitiation for the sins of Arabs, too—as I John 2:2 teaches? Why then do many of the followers of Christ disobey our Master, leaving unregenerate Arabs and Jews to face God without hope for eternal life?

My cultural background has prepared me for the task this exciting study presents. Born and raised in the Middle East, I grew up a child of Druzism, an offshoot of Islam, and received my education in both the Middle East and the United States. Hence I am well aware of the prejudices that have encouraged misunderstandings and resulted in the rooting of a number of myths which I propose to examine in the light of God's written Word.

Chapter One
My Greatest Discovery

Man is a product of his ethnic heritage, whereby he is conditioned to like and to dislike, to accept and to reject, to love and to hate certain things and certain people. Moreover, he has been programmed by his own cultural upbringing to interpret and to internalize his prejudices and pride logically, in a manner that appears to put God on his side.

My religious heritage was received from my mother's family. Her father was head of the Lebanese Druze sect, and my first formal instruction about God was received from my revered grandfather. He taught me to fear God and honor my elders, to be hospitable to stranger and friend alike. As far as I can remember, he never spoke an unkind word to me; his love was unconditional. I have rarely met a man with such a loving and forgiving heart. In other words, he lived his faith. Because of his example and the good training I received from him, the precepts and practices of my childhood religion permeated my total life, and I had no reason to question its claims and commandments.

It is interesting to note that much of the Druze fundamental tenets are founded upon Greek philosophy. For instance, Druze tradition asserts that God created humankind by a spoken word, and that he created a fixed number of individuals which will neither increase nor decrease. This doctrine is supported by the conviction that when a person dies, the soul occupies a new human body by a process of transmigration, called reincarnation. This belief is common to many cultures.

Some maintain that the soul may immediately inhabit either a higher or a lower form of life at the moment of death.

Among the best known proponents of the transmigration of souls was the Greek philosopher Pythagoras, who introduced a philosophical dualism which distinguished between the soul and the body. He also taught that the soul can reside in more than one human body at the same time. This doctrine was later adopted in mythical form by Plato. Such noted philosophers considered the soul an immortal spiritual agent, capable of attaining greater knowledge of good and evil through the purifying process of transmigration.

Druzism also teaches that there is no divine justice apart from reincarnation. The body to which the soul transmigrates upon death is determined by deeds done in the immediate past life. The human soul (Nafs) differs from the spirit (Rouh), in that both man and animal have a body and a spirit, but only man has a soul. Man is composed of three elements: the physical, which is the body; the spirit, which is the blood and life (Hayat); and the soul, which comprises the intellect, the true spiritual life of the individual (Al Jawhar). The spirit and the body cannot be separated, but the soul travels.

Man was created with noble distinctions and keen senses not possessed by animals. Animals strive only to eat, drink, and sleep. Man was created with much higher goals. Since man, through the soul, is immortal, and animals are not, only man will be judged by God in the last day (Hisab). However, Druzism does not believe in a literal hell. When a man is judged by God in the last day, he will simply regret that he did not live in accordance to God's commandments.

The doctrine of reincarnation is only one of many distinctive viewpoints which sharply identify Druzism, as opposed to other monotheistic religious beliefs. Every orthodox Druze embraces humanitarianism and strongly holds to the practice of hospitality, honesty, high morals, and patriotism. All this my grandfather imparted to me through his teaching and his life.

Throughout my childhood, I was exposed to a well-rounded education. My father had studied law at the Sorbonne in Paris,

France, and became the Prosecutor General under the French Mandatory Rule in the late 1920s. Philosophy, politics, arts, history, religion, and other pertinent topics were discussed almost daily at our home, which was crowded with people who needed special favors from my father. Room and board were offered to many who came from afar. Because of this exposure to diverse ideas and to social and international relations, human interaction and religion were my favorite subjects.

After the untimely death of my parents when I was about twelve years old, a relative enrolled me in a Catholic boarding school in East Beirut. In high school I learned about the various religious beliefs and philosophies which were taught at that time. Later on, I decided to enter a private Muslim institution in West Beirut. There I became very fond of my Arabian philosophy professor, who was an atheist. His studies had led him to the conclusion that matter was eternal and self-existing. Therefore, he saw no need to believe in God. He was a nominal Muslim, but felt he should not conceal the abandonment of his religious views.

I was much impressed and influenced by my professor's intellectual ability and charismatic personality, which made it easy for him to sow the seed of doubt in my young and gullible heart. His empirical and analytical mind gave me much meat to chew on, and before long I began to view the idea of God as unscientific and outdated. My own religious convictions were greatly challenged and found to be wanting.

I had never really thought I would come to a point in my life where I would seriously entertain doubts about the reality of God, but I found myself absorbed in one of the greatest mental struggles I was ever to experience. I looked toward heaven and repeatedly asked if God really existed. I sought isolation to meditate upon this burning question, which occupied my mind for a long, long time. Weeks and months went by, but heaven remained silent, or so it seemed.

Although I had fallen under the sway of my professor's opinions, atheism left my inquisitive mind with too many

3

unanswered questions. I was determined to find convincing answers through reason. As I became increasingly aware of the fact that there is no evidence to support the belief that the universe is eternal, I was forced to acknowledge that there must be a powerful and intelligent Being who had created the whole universe and all that is in it. For instance, the fact that he had created a beautiful and orderly world provided an explanation for the rhythm and order and beauty in life that are found everywhere, in spite of man's interference. By a process of logical deduction, my belief in the existence of God was restored and strengthened.

After leaving college, I went to Cairo, Egypt, to seek a future for myself in the entertainment world as a singer and dramatic actor. Cairo was the Hollywood of the Middle East at that time, and since I was blessed with a singing voice and was aspiring to become an actor, I set out to the mecca of the Arabian artists. While in Egypt, I fell in love with the logical teachings of the prophet Muhammed and was almost persuaded to become one of his followers.

Theologically, Islam is Christianity's most skillful and articulate intellectual competitor, claiming to have surpassed and superseded Christianity. It affirms that Muhammed is the last and greatest messenger of God and that the Kur'an is the uncorrupted revelation of the will of Allah. Islam also teaches that the gospel of Christ has been adulterated by the Apostle Paul and other mortal men. The Comforter promised by Jesus Christ had appeared in the person of Muhammed, who came to restore the truth and to correct the polluted narratives of the New Testament. Therefore Muhammed's teachings must replace the gospel of Jesus Christ, and the crescent, a symbol of political power, must be substituted for the cross.

Historically, Islam has been the only world religion to succeed in winning great numbers of converts from Christianity. During the seventh century Islam was propagated by the sword. Spain, North Africa, the Middle East, and southeastern Europe all fell to the followers of Muhammed, who swarmed out of the Arabian Peninsula to sweep the Fertile Crescent.

4

They pushed east as far as the Indus River and west through North Africa to Spain, where they ruled from the eighth to the fifteenth centuries. Arabic was then the Lingua Franca, and much intellectual activity and scientific research in practically every field of learning flourished. The torch of enlightenment then was carried by Arabs, while Europe was enshrouded with darkness. Christianity virtually ceased to exist in the very land where Jesus had walked.

When I immigrated to the United States in 1953, I had to adjust to a completely different way of life, and like so many strangers in a foreign land, I experienced cultural shock. I could not speak English and was unable to communicate even my basic needs. It was difficult to find a job, and when I did find one, I was not able to keep it because of my inability to speak English and my aristocratic upbringing, which discouraged manual labor. Also, American cuisine did not satisfy my Middle Eastern taste—many nights I went to bed hungry and frustrated. I was so lonely for a human touch and felt so utterly alienated from my friends and relatives in Lebanon that I wept bitterly and became deeply depressed.

The turning point in my life came while I was bedridden in 1954 as a result of an automobile crash. At that time, I was enrolled at a state college in Kirksville, Missouri. I had been invited to spend Christmas with some friends living in New York, and four of my college friends offered me a ride to my destination. As we left Kirksville, I fell asleep reciting my prayers in Arabic. Shortly afterward, our car slid under a tractor-trailer and was completely demolished. All four of my friends were killed. When I awoke, I found myself lying in a hospital bed, having been in a coma for two days. God had miraculously rescued me for a specific reason, a reason not revealed to me at that time.

For several months afterward, I prayed fervently, asking God to take my miserable life. I could not understand why he allowed me to suffer under these grueling circumstances, depriving me of the love of my parents and alienating me from my native country. I really wanted to die, but I could not take my own life because of my Druze convictions. My grandfather, who had taught me to fear God and honor my elders, also taught me to refrain from taking any life, for murder and suicide are condemned by God.

Up to that point, I had little respect for or patience with Christian missionaries. I was conditioned to believe that because God was neither begotten nor does he beget, Jesus is not the only Son of God, nor the Savior of the world, nor the Mediator between God and man. He was simply a created man like us. In other words, if Jesus was the Son of God, this logically would imply that God has a wife. In my consideration of the Christian faith, the problem became more difficult for me to comprehend as I attempted to relate the meaning of "Son of God" to the Trinity. Logically, I could not but conclude that Christians were idolaters. It appeared to me that they worshiped three gods and a goddess named Mary.

As a Druze, I was instructed and strongly believed that both the Jews and the idolatrous Christians were cursed by God. As I studied comparative religion and traveled widely, I learned that discrimination and prejudice are not restricted to the Druze religion. Each ethnic and religious group has been programmed to accept certain prejudices as revealed truth.

Because of my Islamic upbringing, I believed in a literal hell and lived in dread of Judgment Day. I grew up with feelings of hostility, doubt, suspicion, insecurity, hate, and anxiety. I was haunted by the fear of death, because I had no certainty that, no matter how hard I tried to please God, I would be saved from his wrath. It was from this perspective that I viewed the world around me when on September 1, 1955, God sent a Christian missionary to visit me.

He invited me to his home near Princeton, New Jersey, where he expounded upon the gospel of Jesus Christ. I heard the dramatic account of the crucifixion again and again. Then suddenly I understood that it was only by Christ's death, the shedding of his blood and bodily resurrection, that I could be forgiven and accepted by God. I wanted so much to be accepted by Almighty God. No one else, since my grandfather's death, had accepted me unconditionally, loved me unconditionally, or given me such a feeling of security.

My new spiritual birth took place on September 11. I remember vividly the tears of repentance that flowed from my weary eyes and the electrifying sensation of joy that filled my aching heart and flooded my soul. I began to praise my Lord and Savior Jesus Christ for bringing me out of utter darkness into his marvelous light, as his Holy Spirit revealed to me "the light of the glorious gospel of Christ . . . for it is the power of God unto salvation to every one that believeth" (II Corinthians 4:4; Romans 1:16). That was my greatest discovery!

After my glorious salvation experience, the Lord Jesus gave me a holy hunger for the Bible, and I began to devour it. As I studied the Word of God like a hungry man seeking bread, or a diver searching for pearls at the bottom of the sea, the Holy Spirit illuminated my mind concerning the meaning of the "Son of God" in relation to the Trinity. As I studied Arabic literature, I discovered a literary expression analogous to "Son of God" in the Christian Bible. The expression *ibn esshaitan,* which in Arabic literally means *son of Satan,* is only figurative and does not imply an actual physical reproduction. Likewise, the title Son of God indicates a unique and supernatural relationship between God and Christ. It does not involve any act or process of procreation.

A careful and diligent examination of the Bible led me further to the understanding that God condemns idolatry and polytheism. No one who is really searching for the true and only living God could fail to realize that the Bible consistently teaches, without apology, that there is *only* one true and living God. There is one God, but there are three distinct personalities: Father, Son, and Holy Spirit. They are eternally and organically the one and only living God. Each person of the Trinity has a unique ministry, which can be appreciated and accepted only by genuine regenerate Christians. However, it has been said that anyone who will try to fully understand the Trinity is bound to lose his mind, but anyone who will deny the Trinity will lose his soul for eternity.

Biblical truths are a striking contrast to the claims of all man-made religions. The Bible tells us that God became flesh in order to redeem all who believe in the death and resurrection of our Lord and Savior Jesus Christ. Any individual who understands that God laid down his life on the cross by his own choice and that he shed his precious blood to atone for the sins of the whole world—that individual will be convicted and convinced by the Holy Spirit of his total depravity.

The doctrine of man's total depravity has been utterly rejected by the Adamic nature, mainly because the natural human ego is reluctant to submit to self-analysis or to the biblical truth concerning that unregenerate condition. It is not pleasant to destroy delusions and expose the deep-rooted sinful attitudes that have served to shield the old nature from reality. However, the Bible describes man as incurably vile. The heart of man is "deceitful above all things, and desperately wicked" (Jeremiah 17:9). Paul confirms the truth taught in Psalms 14:3: "There is none that doeth good, no, not one" (Romans 3:12). In other words, man can no more cure his sinful nature than he can sweeten a pile of manure by pouring out upon it a large bottle of the most expensive perfume.

John Bunyan, author of *Pilgrim's Progress,* once said, "When God showed me John Bunyan as God saw John Bunyan, I no longer confessed I was a sinner, but I confessed that I was sin from the crown of my head to the soles of my feet." To express it differently, our sinful nature does not need to be reformed—it needs to be *transformed* by the new spiritual birth. Our dear Lord told the religious Nicodemus that, "Except a man be born again . . . of water and of the Spirit, he cannot enter into the kingdom of God" (John 3:3, 5).

Parenthetically, there are many Middle Eastern customs of which western cultures are not aware, as is the case in reverse. As one searches the Scriptures, some are easily discovered while others remain hidden from view. For instance, one such custom is highlighted in a conversation between the Lord Jesus and Nicodemus—a Pharisee and respected ruler of the Jews. "The same came to Jesus by night" (John 3:2), not because he was afraid to come during the daylight hours, as is the contention of many. This is not the case at all. Actually, it was and still is customary for many Arabs and Jews to visit their relatives and friends after the evening meal. This custom was not originated by the Semitic peoples, but by God himself. The Lord visited Adam and Eve "in the cool of the day" (Genesis 3:8).

Man will never be able to solve the predicament of his total depravity, nor restore his relationship with God, by relying on his puny wisdom or by clinging to ethnic and religious prejudices and the dogmas programmed into him. Man must come to the foot of the cross and give his total life to Christ. There he will obtain mercy and eternal salvation, and with the regenerating power of the Holy Spirit, his computer (his mind) will be reprogrammed. After our salvation, our Lord requires our obedience. He wants us to live for him, but no Christian can live for Christ unless he is willing to die for him. Christ is the God of love, and if we love him, we will obey him unto death. The Lord said, "Be thou faithful unto death" (Revelation 2:10).

Millions of born-again Christians have already died and are still dying for their uncompromising faith, because of the world's hatred of God's Son, the Lord and Savior Jesus Christ (Matthew 10:22, 24:9; Luke 6:22; John 7:7, 15:18-23, 17:14). They have been stoned to death, thrown to the beasts, beheaded, chained and imprisoned, crucified, sawn in two, put to death with the sword, and burned at the stake. Such Christians were individuals "of whom the world was not worthy" (Hebrews 11:36-38). "The time cometh," Jesus said, "that whosoever killeth you will think that he doeth God service" (John 16:2). All those people were martyred for trying to propagate the gospel of Jesus Christ—not for any evil deed they had done.

We must remember that our dear Lord is the chief target of persecution. Paul discovered this truth on the road to Damascus when the Lord said, "Saul, Saul, why persecutest thou me?" (Acts 9:4). We are not persecuted because we hold strong views about various religious or denominational beliefs. We are persecuted because Christ dwells in all people who have been baptized with the Holy Spirit through their faith in Christ Jesus. "Now if any man have not the Spirit of Christ, he is none of his. . . . For by one Spirit are we all baptized into one body, whether we be Jews or Gentiles" (Romans 8:9; I Corinthians 12:13). If Christ is the chief target, then his followers are the beneficiaries. Suffering confirms the believer as a son of God (Hebrews 12:7), promotes his character, and cleanses him in the blood of the Lamb (Revelation 7:14).

As a born-again disciple of Christ, I have been learning to love what God loves and to hate what God hates. God loves the human race, but he hates evil deeds and false doctrines (John 3:16; Revelation 2:15). In fact, I am also learning to think and act objectively. As the Holy Spirit continues his work of sanctification in my heart, he is rendering me able to consistently view all my fellow men with the compassion and love that can come only from my Lord and my God, Jesus Christ himself!

Chapter Two
Heritage of the Arabs

It is bewildering to realize that God can take ordinary people from all walks of life and use them to accomplish his purposes. The Bible is replete with instances of the children of Israel being used by God. However, less attention has been given to God's historical use of Arabs. God desires that many of them should come to know him today in a personal way and be used by him, as some were used by him in the past.

The Faith of Caleb
(Caleb is Ghalib in Arabic, meaning conqueror.)

Caleb and Joshua were two of the twelve spies sent by Moses into the land of Canaan to bring back a report to the wandering children of Israel. With staunch faith in God's promises, Caleb urged the people to go up and take the land. But the people refused to obey for fear of the enemy and as a result, wandered aimlessly in the wilderness of the Sinai Peninsula for forty years, until a new generation could enter the land of Canaan. God rewarded Caleb by making him a leader and giving him the land of Hebron (Joshua 14:6-15): "But my servant Caleb, because he had another spirit with him, and hath followed me fully, him will I bring into the land whereinto he went; and his seed shall possess it" (Numbers 14:24).

We read of the aged Caleb years later, still vigorous and faithful in his walk with God, and still determined to claim his inheritance in the land of Israel. At eighty-five years of age, Caleb asked Joshua for permission to drive out the Anakims.

Joshua was stirred by Caleb's courage and obedience and gave him the land around Hebron.

The story of Caleb and the role he played in the conquest of the Promised Land is well known. What is not well known is that Caleb was descended from people usually associated with the Arabs. Caleb was the son of Jephunneh, a Kennizite from the tribe of Kenaz. Esau, Jacob's brother, became the father of many tribes, one of which was that of Eliphaz. The mother of Eliphaz was Adah, a Hittite. Kenaz is the son of Eliphaz and the progenitor of the Kennizites. So Caleb is actually an Edomite, a descendant of Esau. Caleb was proselytized into the tribe of Judah through the intermarriage of his Gentile ancestors. Imagine, a man in the line of modern Arabs was a man of God, leading the tribe of Judah, from which was born our Lord and Savior Jesus Christ (Numbers 13:6).

It is also recorded that Othniel, Caleb's brother, became the first judge of Israel, driving out Cushan-rishathaim, the king of Mesopotamia. Othniel married Achsah, the daughter of Caleb, as a reward for liberating the area around Debir (about 12 miles southwest of Hebron). Calebite settlements flourished greatly in and around Hebron and Debir. Much later, David occupied these Calebite neighborhoods, including Hebron, where he was first crowned king. Absalom also resorted to Hebron during his revolt against David, his father, because of the independent attitude of the Calebites toward the people of Judah. The descendants of Caleb were eventually driven northward toward Jerusalem during the time of king Nebuchadnezzar's attacks, prior to the Babylonian captivity.

The Counsel of Shu'aib

Moses needed to be mentally and spiritually prepared before he could receive God's law. Difficult and unforeseen circumstances were made ready by God, and Shu'aib was sent to assist Moses with his task. After crossing the Red Sea, Moses judged disputes among the murmuring people from morning until night. This impossible mission fatigued Moses and also wearied the people, since there was only one judge for the entire nation. Shu'aib saw and understood the problem and counseled Moses to teach God's laws and statutes to many judges, and then place those judges over groups of one thousand, one hundred, fifty, and ten. The judicial task would be streamlined, made more efficient and smooth, both for Moses and for the people. Moses saw that Shu'aib's counsel was wise and practical, and he saw the need to become an intermediary between the people and God.

Shu'aib is Arabic for Jethro, Moses' father-in-law, also known as Reuel. Interesting information can be gleaned about Jethro from a study of genealogy. Jethro was a priest in the tribe of Midian—a Keturahite Arab. After Sarah's death Abraham took a wife named Keturah, with whom he had six sons: Zimran, Jokshan, Medan, Midian, Ishbak, and Shuah. Abraham sent those sons away to the east with gifts, where they became progenitors of Arab tribes (Genesis 25:1-6). Near Eastern tradition holds Keturah to be the ancestress of the Turks.

Moses married Zipporah, Jethro's daughter. In Numbers 12:1, Miriam and Aaron made an outcry against Moses for marrying a black woman. However, God was not angry with them for criticizing the woman, but for contesting Moses' authority (Numbers 12:2-16). God allows intercultural marriage as long as it does not lead to idolatry and polytheistic worship; and as long as both husband and wife are willing to adjust to cultural shock, remaining faithful to the Lord Jesus and to each other. Otherwise, it would be better to marry from one's own ethnic background.

The Bible teaches that Zipporah is a Cushite, Keturahite, and Midianite Arab. How could that be so? Scripture provides the answer. One of Keturah's sons, Jokshan, had descendants named Sheba and Dedan, mentioned in other parts of the Bible. For instance, in Ezekiel's prophecy against Tyre, God says, "The men of Dedan were thy merchants; many isles were the merchandise of thine hand: they brought thee for a present horns of ivory and ebony" (Ezekiel 27:15). These men of Dedan and Sheba appear to have settled around the Persian

Gulf and the Arabian Sea, and there they became caravan merchants and traders.

However, in I Chronicles 1:9, we are told that Raamah, a son of Cush, had two sons, Sheba and Dedan. The mystery of the Cushite Zipporah might be solved by the fact that Abraham's wife Keturah was a Cushite descendant of Raamah. All the sons of Keturah, then, would be of Abrahamic and Cushite blood. Keturah's grandsons, Sheba and Dedan, would be, in a manner of speaking, sons or descendants of Raamah, but after many generations. Genealogies are sometimes stated in this way. Miriam and Aaron thus referred to Zipporah as "the Ethiopian," or a Cushite woman, perhaps because of this genealogical connection with Cush.

Cush was the oldest son of Ham, the son of Noah. I believe that Cush was created black from two white parents. He was the progenitor of the black race and the founder of Ethiopia. Ethiopia was known to the Greeks as Africa. The Cushites intermixed with other races and may have been semitized after they arrived in the Sudan. This may very well be the reason for the various shades of blackness that exist in the Near East. Jeremiah 13:23 seems to support these views: "Can the Ethiopian change his skin?"

These Midianite Arabs played a large role in the history of Israel. After Moses' trying experience as national judge, and after he had received the wise and practical counsel of Jethro (Shu'aib), he met God on Sinai and received the law. Jethro played a large part in God's prophetic plan. Likewise, Jethro's son Hobab was used by the Lord to guide the children of Israel during their wandering in the wilderness. As Moses said, "Thou mayest be to us instead of eyes" (Numbers 10:29-36). So the Midianite Arabs were instrumental in preparing Moses for meeting God on Mount Sinai and in guiding the children of Israel in the land, which the Midianites knew very well.

King Saul (In Arabic, Talootu, means *tallness.* King Saul evidently was a tall man.) showed kindness to the Midianites on his way to do battle with the Amalekites, descendants of Esau (Genesis 36:12). "And Saul said unto the Kenites, Go, depart, get you down from among the Amalekites, lest I destroy you with them: for ye shewed kindness to all the children of Israel, when they came up out of Egypt. So the Kenites departed from among the Amalekites" (I Samuel 15:6). In the book of Judges we are told that yet another name for Midianites is Kenites and that they attached themselves to the children of Israel and lived with them (Judges 1:16). These loyal Arabians left "the city of palm trees" and went to the wilderness with the children of Israel under the faithfulness of God. Another branch of the Midianite tribe is known as the Rechabite (I Chronicles 2:55). This tribe became so respected in Israel for its faith in God and ascetic life that Rechabites were accorded places of honor in the worship of Jehovah and were used as examples of faithfulness to the rest of the men of Judah in Jerusalem (Jeremiah 35). History tells us that they may well have become scribes in Israel, incorporated into the tribe of Levi for priestly duties. Jewish tradition asserts that Rechabites gave their daughters in marriage to the Levites and that their children ministered in the temple.

The Lebanese king of Tyre materially assisted David by sending cedar wood and skilled workmen to build the palace in Jerusalem (II Samuel 5:11). Likewise, Hiram furnished the required cedar timber for the temple of Solomon (I Kings 5). In return for Hiram's good deeds, Solomon gave him "twenty cities in the land of Galilee" (I Kings 9:11). It is interesting to note that the Tyrians taught the Jewish sailors the art of bringing gold from Ophir (I Kings 9:26-28). Eusebius, the Christian theologian and historian, relates that Hiram, in addition to helping Israel with many good deeds, gave his daughter in marriage to Solomon.

God also used Zarephath, the Lebanese widow, to host prophet Elijah during the latter part of the great famine (I Kings 17:8-10). Furthermore, it is possible that some or all of the wise men who came from the east to worship the Lord Jesus and give him gifts were Arabs (Matthew 2:1-12). Many Arabian tribes that settled in the Arabian Peninsula and along the Persian Gulf intermingled with Jews and were proselytized by them (see Acts 2:11). Those people were also famous for frankincense and myrrh. The Queen of Sheba (modern Yemen) brought similar gifts to Solomon (I Kings 10:1-10; II Chronicles 9:1-9).

These are but a few examples of God's use of Arabs and their contributions to the children of Israel. However, these biblical truths are seldom taught in western Bible colleges and seminaries.

Arab Genealogy

"And as for Ishmael, I have heard thee: Behold, I have blessed him, and will make him fruitful, and will multiply him exceedingly; twelve princes shall he beget, and I will make him a great nation" (Genesis 17:20, 21:17-19). Most people think of Ishmael as the original forebear of the Arabs. Likewise, the Kur'an links the Arabs to Ishmael. This information comes down to us by word of mouth from the pre-Muhammedan law of blood revenge, which required every Muslim to trace his ancestry back four generations in order to defend the family honor. This law of blood revenge is an Old Testament tradition: "eye for eye, tooth for tooth" (Leviticus 24:20). However, it would be most interesting to trace the genealogy of this man, whom God promised to bless in physical wealth and to make of him a great nation.

Abraham's lineage is generally known, but that of Hagar is not. Hagar, meaning *flight*, was a concubine of Abraham. Although we consider Sarah's conduct wrong and sinful when she gave her Egyptian maid to her husband for the purpose of procreation, her action was in full accord with the custom of her day. Contracted marriages during that time gave a barren wife the legal right to offer her handmaid (bondwoman) to her husband in order to obtain an heir. In fact, four of the twelve tribes of Israel were born of Zilpah and Bilhah, the slaves of Jacob's wives, Rachel and Leah (Genesis 30:1-13).

Ishmael was the first son of Abraham and Hagar, the Egyptian handmaid of Sarah. Hagar gave birth to Ishmael when Abraham was eighty-six years old (Genesis 16:16). With this in mind, let me briefly try to offer a reason for the chronic turmoil that exists between Arabs and Jews. The predicament was initiated by the three characters in Genesis 16 and 21.

Abraham, Sarah, and Hagar had lived peacefully and happily under the same roof. But that coveted lifestyle changed abruptly. Although God had promised Abraham an heir (Genesis 15:4), Sarah was able to persuade her husband to help God work out the fulfillment of the promise. When Abraham submitted to his wife's suggestion and took Hagar as a secondary wife (Genesis 16:3), he willingly disregarded the divine promise and resorted to human contrivance.

From that time, tragic consequences have multiplied, and matters have grown worse by the moment between Arabs and Jews. Mutual dislike and jealousy set the two women against each other, and Abraham could not alleviate his household problem. Sarah dealt so harshly with Hagar that she could no longer bear the suffering. Her persecution led her to flee in desperation to the wilderness, where God appeared to her in person and commanded that she return to her mistress.

His heartening words comforted Hagar greatly. She was exhilarated by the realization that she had been in the presence of the Almighty God, who promised to multiply and bless her descendants. Hagar submitted to God's will and waited patiently under the most grueling circumstances. In fact, she is one of the best examples of total *submission* to the will of God. *Islam* means exactly that in Arabic.

It is not unreasonable to assume that the two mothers inoculated Ishmael and Isaac with the hate they felt for each other. Perhaps the two sons acquired their pride and prejudice from their mothers, while Abraham, with grief, watched the disintegration of his family. Only the Lord Jesus is able to reconcile a remnant of these blood relatives, and he is planning to do just that at his second coming (Isaiah 19:25).

Ishmael (Isma-El) means *whom God hears*. God heard the heartaches of Abraham and Hagar concerning their son and gave them several promises. In addition to the promises given to Abraham in Genesis 17:20 and 21:13, God also gave Hagar five promises in Genesis 16:10-12.

1. *"I will multiply thy seed exceedingly."*

God has most certainly fulfilled this promise. He gave Ishmael twelve sons and one daughter, Mahalath, whom Esau took as his wife (Genesis 28:9). God has blessed the Ishmaelites with more than three million square miles of rich land. They may constitute most of the population of Algeria, Morocco, Tunisia, Bahrain, Egypt, Iraq, Jordan, Kuwait, Lebanon, Libya, Oman, Qatar, Saudi Arabia, Sudan, Syria, Yemen, Abu Dhabi, Dubai, and Aden-prot. They have more than half of the world's proven oil reserves and control the most strategic location on earth: a pathway linking three great continents—Africa, Europe, and Asia.

2. *"And he will be a wild man;"*

This might refer to the fact that no nation could tame the Arabs. On the other hand, Ishmael represents the Adamic nature, as Galatians 4:23 teaches. Man can be controlled either by the Holy Spirit, through faith in Christ Jesus, or by his total depravity.

Moreover, God is using the Arabs as a thorn in the flesh of all concerned, particularly Israel, in order to fulfill his prophetic plan (see Chapter 4).

3. *"His hand will be against every man;"*

This could mean that the Arabs may never become united, due to Abraham's sin of disobedience (Genesis 17:17). Arabian history attests to this very fact.

The Arabs have many good qualities. However, although they respect strength, they have no compassion for weakness. For instance, they reject the main teachings of Christ: "Love your enemies, bless them that curse you, do good to them that hate you, and pray for them which despitefully use you, and persecute you" (Matthew 5:44).

4. *"and every man's hand against him;"*

It has been said that when the Arabs are not at war with an enemy, they will always be at war with one another. They are probably the least liked and the most misunderstood of nations. Foreign exploiters have taken advantage of this perceived weakness to accomplish their economic and political desires.

5. *"and he shall dwell in the presence of all his brethren."*

It is interesting to note that Arabs have not been up-rooted from their countries. God dispersed the Jews for their unbelief (Ezekiel 36:19). He also destroyed Babylon and said that "it shall never be inhabited" (Isaiah 13:20); and in the same verse, "neither shall the Arabian pitch tent there." The prophecy was fulfilled concerning the utter destruction of Babylon and the dispersion of the Jews, but the Arabs will remain rooted in their lands until the Lord Jesus returns to this earth. Babylon was destroyed by Medo-Persia under Cyrus in 538 B.C. (Jeremiah 51:62), while Ishmael not only lived but also "died in the presence of all his brethren" (Genesis 25:18).

Ishmael is the seed of Abraham, but was the son of the Egyptian bondwoman, Hagar (Genesis 21:13), and according to Jewish tradition, children inherit their mother's nationality. Hagar could be traced to Mizraim, the second son of Ham (Genesis 10:6); Mizraim founded Egypt after Ham settled in that part of the world. In fact, the Bible identifies Egypt as "the land of Ham" (Psalms 105:23, 27, 106:22). The Hagarites, living in eastern Palestine, were the tribe with which Reuben made war during the reign of Saul (I Chronicles 5:10, 18-20).

Ishmael, the reputed ancestor of the prophet Muhammed, married an Egyptian (Genesis 21:21). Arab tradition connects Ishmael to Joktan by the marriage of a daughter of Jurhum. Jurhum was called a "son" of Joktan. According to Arabic and Hebrew tradition, "son" means *descendant*. The tribe of Jurhum guarded the Kaabah in Mecca until they were expelled by the Ishmaelites.

Abraham's seed through Isaac is better known than his seed through Hagar and through Keturah, whom he married after Sarah's death (Genesis 25:1). It is amazing that these biblical facts have been so generally overlooked by many Bible scholars. We are often told that Ishmael is the progenitor of the Arabs, but the Bible traces the Arabs to Eber, a great-grandson of Shem, one of the three sons of Noah (Genesis 10:21-30).

Eber had two sons, Peleg and Joktan (Genesis 10:25). The Arabs originated from Joktan, the Hebrews from Peleg. Both peoples and their respective languages derive their meaning from the root word *Eber*. According to a Hebrew and Chaldee dictionary, *Arab* comes from a primary root word meaning "to lie in wait, to ambush, to mingle and intermix, to give or be security, to engage and meddle with, to occupy, to undertake close association, to be pleasant, to grow dusky at sundown, to be darkened toward evening."

This statement briefly describes the nomadic tribal life and character of Arabs very well. Arabs are called Semitic people mainly because they descended from Shem. However, in Europe and the Western world, the Semite has come to possess an exclusive Jewish connotation. But on account of the wide and long dispersion of Jews and their intermarriages with the Gentiles, they have not been able to keep their ethnic purity. On the other hand, Arabs have been able to preserve their cultural traits and were given the opportunity by God to conserve more of their traditional peculiarities. Therefore, they may be considered the best representatives of the Semitic people socially, linguistically, psychologically, and geographically, due to their monotonous uniformity of desert life and the fact that they have never been uprooted from their habitat.

Joktan was the father of the thirteen Arabian tribes (Genesis 10:26-29). The name Joktan, or Kahtan, as the Arabs prefer to call him, comes from a Hebrew word meaning *small in stature*. He has been clearly identified by reliable theologians and historians as the father of the thirteen biblical and historical tribes occupying the Arabian Peninsula. The original boundaries were stated in the Word of God: "And their dwelling was from Mesha, as thou goest unto Sephar a mount of the east" (Genesis 10:30). Mesha is located toward the western boundary, and Sephar (Zafari) is the modern seaport of southern Arabia, located east of Yemen.

Kahtan, or Kaht, means *drought*. Arabian tradition asserts that as Joktan crossed over the Arabian desert on one of his nomadic journeys, he suffered from starvation and thirst. To this day Arabs are called "sons of Kahtan", and the meaning of Eber is *to cross over the desert*. Although Arabs are well known for telling fables and associating names with meaningful experiences, this is immaterial to the fact that the Joktanites colonized the Arabian Peninsula, stretching from Yemen in the south to Mecca on the northwest, and almost all the southern coast eastward, going far inland.

Arab Tribes

Almodad (Genesis 10:26; I Chronicles 1:20)

The name in Hebrew means *the friend of God*. According to Ibn Khaldûn (1332–1406), considered the greatest Arabian historian, Almodad, or El-Mudad, was the reputed father-in-law of Ishmael. The Arabs call his descendants the tribe of Morad. This tribe, very friendly and hospitable, especially to strangers, lived in a mountainous region in the Arabian peninsula.

Dikla (Genesis 10:27; I Chronicles 1:21)

The meaning in Hebrew is *palm tree*, and the cognate word in Arabic means *a palm tree abounding with fruit*. Hence, Dikla, or Kiklah, is a part of Arabia containing many palm trees. Dikla's descendants occupied a portion of Yemen, to the east of Hijaz.

Abimael (Genesis 10:28; I Chronicles 1:22)

The name in Hebrew, Abimelech, means *father of a king*, or *father-king*. The Arabs had many heads of tribes called kings. Abimael was the founder of the Arabian tribe called Mael, or Mali. The Jews also called some of their kings' fathers Abimelech.

Hadoram (Genesis 10:27; I Chronicles 1:21)

The name in Greek is Aduram, or Adoram, meaning *fire worshippers*. Very little is known about this Arabian tribe. However, they probably merged with Hazarmaveth, becoming known as Hadramawt, in Arabic.

Havilah (Genesis 10:29)

Cush also had a son named Havilah (Genesis 10:7). It seems that a tribe carrying that name formed the westernmost colony of Cush along southern Arabia and that the Joktanites were an earlier colonization. It is commonly thought that the district of Khawlan in Yemen was the abode of this Arabian tribe. Khawlan is located between the cities of San'a and Hijaz in the northwestern portion of Yemen. The Arabs believe that Khawlan was a descendant of Kahtan (Joktan). The district of Khawlan is a fertile territory with plenty of water.

Hazarmaveth (Genesis 10:26)

In Hebrew, Asarmoth means *court of death*. The name is preserved almost literally in the Arabian province of the southern peninsula. It is believed that Joktan settled in Yemen. The province of Hazarmaveth, or Hadramawt in Arabic, is located east of modern Yemen. Its capital is Shibam, and its chief seaports are Mirbat, Zafari (Sephar), and Kisheem, from whence a great trade was carried on in ancient times with India and Africa.

Jobab (Genesis 10:29; I Chronicles 1:23)

In Hebrew the word means *a place in the desert*. Jobab is a district in the Arabian desert, and it is difficult to find more information about this tribe. It is assumed that some intermarriage occurred with the descendants of Esau (Genesis 36:33). One of the kings of Edom is Jobab, and the Septuagint identifies him as the Patriarch Job, whose father was Zerah, the son of Esau.

Jerah (Genesis 10:26; I Chronicles 1:20)

The word means *new moon*. The descendants of Jerah have lived near the Red Sea and Yemen. Many great Arabian poets came from this tribe. The moon, when near the sun, shows a narrow rim of light and perhaps gave the poets much inspiration.

Obal (Genesis 10:28)

Obal, or Ebal, means *naked*. Perhaps this tribe occupied a part of southern Arabia, but this is difficult to prove.

Ophir (Genesis 10:29; I Chronicles 1:23)

Sofir is the Coptic word for India. It is most interesting to note that this Arabian tribe founded India. Sophir, or Sophira, is the name used by Josephus (37−95 A.D.), the renowned Jewish historian, and the Septuagint positively concurs with Josephus that Ophir was a part of India. Furthermore, Arabian historians translated the word Ophir as India. The Bible describes Ophir as very wealthy, with gold and precious stones, and relates that the Arabs shared their wealth with others (I Kings 9:28, 10:11; Isaiah 13:12), one characteristic of the early Semitic lifestyle.

Sheba (Genesis 10:28)

Sheba means *wine-red* or *brown*. The Arabic verb *Seba* means *altered* by the sun or by a fever, turning a person red. This may be the earliest designation for the Red Man. A queen from this tribe came to Solomon's court and exchanged gifts with the king of Israel (I Kings 10:1-13). The people of Sheba are brown-red from the heat of the sun. Sheba has been identified as Yemen.

Sheleph (Genesis 10:26; I Chronicles 1:20)

The word means *drawing out* or *plucking*. The ancient division of Yemen is called Sulaf or Selfia. The tribe of Shelif, or Shulaf, has been recognized by Arab historians as belonging to the Yemen. The modern descendants of this tribe are found in the southern Arabian district of Selfia.

Uzal (Genesis 10:27; I Chronicles 1:21)

This means *beautiful trees*. Uzal, or Awzal, is the capital of Yemen, but the name was later on changed to San'a. The Sabaean (Yemen) society was highly developed technically, as witnessed by the remains of a great dam at Marib, located east of San'a, the center of a large irrigation system.

Further probing into these names yields interesting historical information. The descendants of Havilah are found in the area of Khawlan in Yemen. It is a fertile territory with plenty of water. The area of Havilah referred to in Genesis 2 is said to be rich in gold (Genesis 2:11-12). The descendants of Hazer-maveth are also in the Yemen area of the southern Arabian Peninsula and are known as Hadramawt. Their area includes the port of Zafari, the biblical Sephar. In ancient times a great trade was carried on with India and Africa from this port. The frankincense and myrrh from this region are still known today. Therefore, it is easy to suppose that it was the gold, myrrh, and frankincense of these Arab regions that were carried by the Magi and that the Magi were Arab men of wisdom, acting as representatives of their peoples to acknowledge their rightful Lord and Savior, Jesus Christ.

Tertullian (160–230 A.D.) said that the Magi were Arabs. The Eastern churches teach that the wise men arrived in Jerusalem with an extremely large retinue. Zoroaster taught that in the latter days a star would herald the coming of a mighty redeemer, and tradition holds that twelve of the most devout Magi were chosen to watch for that star. Night after night they washed in pure water, prayed, and watched. At last the star appeared in the form of a young child bearing a cross, and a voice then told them to proceed to Judea.

The gifts to the Christ Child, including gold, myrrh, and frankincense, are held to be the kind of gifts Abraham had given to the sons of Keturah (Genesis 25:6). The queen of Sheba, known as Bilkees, presented these same kinds of gifts to Solomon when she came to hear his wisdom (I Kings 10:1-10). In a psalm foreshadowing Solomon and the Messiah, the gift of Arab gold is foretold: "And he shall live, and to him be given of the gold of Sheba: prayer also shall be made for him continually; and daily shall he be praised" (Psalm 72:15).

Ishmael is descended from Hebrew and Arabic lineage. Tradition tells us that Ishmael's wife, also from Egypt, descended from the tribe of Beni Mudad, or the sons of El-Mudad, the Arabian tribe founded by the friend of God, Almodad, the son of Joktan (Genesis 10:26). God promised Ishmael twelve princes:

Massa (Genesis 25:14) means *present* or *tribute*. He was the progenitor of the Masani tribe, which lived in eastern Arabia near the border of Babylonia. In Proverbs 30:1, some hold the proper reading to be "Agur the Massite," who lived in the area of the Masani; others maintain the reading to be the "Lemuel" of Proverbs 31.

Mibsam (Genesis 25:13) means *sweet odor*, from which the word *balsam* is derived. This tribe settled in the district of Mecca, where a fresh fragrance pervades the surroundings.

Mishma (Genesis 25:14) signifies *hearing* or *report*. The Masamani tribe, called Beni-Misma, lived in the province of Arabia. It has been said that the Masamanis spent their time telling fables and reporting current news.

Naphish (Genesis 25:15) means *refreshment*. Naphish merged with the Hagarenes and went southward to the province of Hejer, near Arabia. This tribe was known for hospitality and friendliness.

Kedar (Genesis 25:13) means *black-skinned*. Kedar settled on the northwest part of the Arabian Peninsula and the confines of Palestine (Isaiah 21:13-17). These Arabs were fierce fighters and great merchants, with lambs, rams, camels, sheep, and goats. A wandering tribe, the people lived in black tents made of camels' hair. The Bible calls them "princes of Kedar" (Ezekiel 27:21). *Arab* is a Semitic word derived from Eber, meaning *desert* or *wilderness*, a biblical description of the early nomadic tribes.

Kedemah (Genesis 25:15) means *eastward*. This tribe settled in eastern Arabia. Acts 17:26 describes the sovereignty of God and the way he determines where every human being should be born.

Abdeel (Genesis 25:13) means *miracle of God*. He is said to be the ancestor of prophet Muhammed. According to Arab tradition, Abdeel was the twenty-first generation before the prophet.

Dumah (Genesis 25:14) means *silence*. Gesenius (1786–1842), a Hebrew scholar, said that this tribe settled in Doomat-el-Jendel in the northwestern region of Arabia.

Nebajoth (Genesis 25:13), meaning *height*, was the oldest son of Ishmael. This tribe, identified with the Nabathaeans, was neighbor to the Arabian clan of Kedar (Isaiah 60:7). The Nabat inhabited the land *beyn-en-nahrein, between* the Tigris and the Euphrates, the Mesopotamia and Chaldea of ancient times (modern Iraq). The people also were called Syro-Chaldaeans. The Arabs apply the name Nabat to Syria. In fact, the Arabian historian El-Mes'oodee says, "The Syrians are the same as the Nabataeans. The Nimrods were the kings of the Syrians, whom the Arabs called Nabataeans." According to Arab historians, the Chaldaeans are the same as the Syrians, and the Nabataeans founded the city of Babylon. The inhabitants of Nineveh were a part of those the Arabs called Nabeet, or Syrians, a pastoral people with great knowledge of agriculture, astronomy, medicine, science, and the arts. Perhaps through intermarriage with Cushite groups, the race of the Chaldaeans sprang from Nabajoth, or Nabaioth. This gives further credence to the idea that the Magi were of Arab lineage, because of the renowned abilities of the Chaldaeans in astronomy and astrology (Daniel 2:2).

Jetur (Genesis 25:15) means *nomadic camp.* Jetur is associated with the tribe that lived near Ituraea in southern Lebanon, over which Philip the Tetrarch ruled when the Word of God came to John the Baptist in the wilderness (Luke 3:1-2). Arabian historians assert that Jetur founded Ituraea, located on the northern border of Palestine. Its capital city was Chalchis, and its chief religious center was Heliopolis (modern Baalbek) in Lebanon.

Hadar (Genesis 25:15), meaning *chamber,* or Hadad, meaning *sharp* or *fierce*—this tribe lived near the border of the Syrian desert, and it should not be identified with the Hadad who descended from Esau (I Kings 11:14).

Tema (Genesis 25:15) means *on the south.* Job spoke of this people in parabolic fashion (Job 6:19), and Isaiah 21:14 mentioned their good deeds toward the hungry and thirsty, characteristic of the Arab lifestyle. Tema, or Teyma, is located in Syria between Wadi el-Kura and Damascus.

Ishmael was Semitic through his father and Hamitic through his mother. He married an Egyptian girl, but this second infusion of Hamitic blood into the progenitors of the Arab nation and the six sons of Keturah by Abraham have been generally neglected by many Bible scholars. The deficiency displayed when it comes to biblical and historical truths concerning the Arabs is remarkable. However, this is immaterial to the fact that the peoples of the Arabian Peninsula are certainly Joktanites, and their colonization of southern Arabia has been proven indisputably. Joktan's sons settled and colonized the whole of the southern Arabian Peninsula, stretching from Yemen in the south to Mecca in Saudi Arabia on the northwest, and along nearly the whole of the southern coast eastward and far inland, as was stated before.

Biblical Sheba (Seba), attained greatness during the time of Joktan. Southwestern Arabia, which included San'a (Uzal), Seba (Sheba), and Hadramawt (Hazarmaveth), formed the principal kingdom in which settlements and colonizations of the Arabian Joktanites were established. They also lived northward in Heereh (Iraq) and Ghassan, near Damascus.

The Joktanites intermarried with the Canaanites, Assyrians, Chaldaeans, Cushites, and others. The Ishmaelites intermarried, also, with the Joktanites, Canaanites, Edomites, Moabites, Ammonites and others. In fact, all races have gone through blood infusion through intermarriage, and as a result, it is not possible to trace any pure human race.

Ishmael's only daughter, Mahalath, or Bashemath, became one of the three wives of Esau, the brother of Jacob (Genesis 28:9; and 36:3). All Arabs and Jews not only are blood brothers, born of the same father, Eber, but all also are the physical seed of Abraham. After Sarah's death, "Abraham took a wife, and her name was Keturah" (Genesis 25:1).

These are Abraham's children through Keturah:
Ishbak (Genesis 25:2; I Chronicles 1:32) means *leaving behind*. He was the progenitor of a tribe of northern Arabia in the valley of Sabak, located in Benee-Temeen, in Nejd, from the great desert of Yensoo'ah to the sands of Yebreen, not far from the Persian Gulf.

Jokshan (Genesis 25:3) means *fowler.* This tribe settled on the borders of Palestine. Jokshan's sons were Sheba and Dedan, from whom the Druze sect may have descended (see "Western Alliance" in Chapter 3).

Medan (Genesis 25:2) means *contention.* This tribe may have merged with Ishmaelite tribes and settled in Arabia on the eastern shore of the Persian Gulf. An early supposition is that Medan merged with Midian; God used the Midianites and the Ishmaelites to bring Joseph "into Egypt" (Genesis 37:36). The Medanites, Midianites, and Ishmaelites were related by blood infusion through intermarriage. Perhaps for this reason, their names have been used interchangeably in the Bible.

Shuah (Genesis 25:2) means *pit.* This tribe may have settled in the Persian Gulf, but very little is known about it.

Zimran (Genesis 25:2) means *sung* or *celebrated.* These people settled near the Red Sea, west of Mecca, after migrating from Yemen, and then came into possession of Zabram, a district of Ethiopia. Some historians contend that Zimran may be identified with the modern Beni Omran. This tribe's descendants have not been clearly identified, apart from the fact that Zimran was the eldest son of Abraham and Keturah (I Chronicles 1:32).

Midian (Genesis 25:2) means *strife.* He was the progenitor of the Midianites. They settled in the desert of the northern Arabian Peninsula and extended southward along the eastern shore of the Gulf of Eyleh. They also lived northward along the eastern borders of Palestine and toward the Sinai Peninsula, where Moses led the flock of Jethro, his father-in-law. The Midianites are Abrahamic Arabs. During the time of Joseph, the Midianites were closely associated with the Ishmaelites (Genesis 37:25, 27, 28, 36). They were related not only through Abraham but also through intermarriage. In Judges 8:24, the Midianites seem to be called Ishmaelites.

We have already seen that all the Arab tribes can be traced back to Joktan (Kahtan). They also can be traced to Abraham, and they, as well as the children of Israel, constitute his descendants. It is assumed that many Arabs have been saved by faith, both before and after Abraham. The Bible records God's blessings on them. The Lord Jesus appeared to Hagar and had much compassion on her, (Genesis 16:7-13; and 21:17-20). God will elect unto salvation anyone who cries out for mercy and believes in the claims of Christ by faith (Galatians 3:8). Hagar had great faith in the Lord and God of Abraham. She was an obedient servant, and because she had had a genuine personal encounter with the Lord Jesus, it is believed that she was saved. She even called his name, Elroi, meaning, "Thou God seest me" (Genesis 16:13).

Tribal Lifestyle

Early Semitic tribes lived in tents made of black goat skin. In Arabic they are called *beit sha'ar*, meaning *house of hair*. Solomon referred to them as "the tents of Kedar" (Song 1:5). Kedar, meaning *black-skinned*, was an Arabian tribe living in black tents made of camel or goat skin. The Hebrew word for *beit* is *bavith*, literally meaning *shelter*. The English equivalent is *house* or *home*. Tents also are made of waterproof sackcloth, a coarse heavy fabric, for protection against sand storms and extreme temperatures. People such as Abraham and David, who walked faithfully with God, lived in tents because they knew they were sojourners and strangers upon the earth (Hebrews 11:9-13).

In fact, both believers and unbelievers lived in tents during the time of Adam and afterward. Jabal "was the father of such as dwell in tents" (Genesis 4:20). Abraham "pitched his tent" near Bethel (Genesis 12:8), and "David, the Ark, and Israel, and Judah, abide in tents" (II Samuel 11:11). The Arabs lived in tents for centuries before and after the destruction of Babylon. God said that Babylon "shall never be inhabited . . . neither shall the Arabian pitch tent there" (Isaiah 13:20). Most Jews do not live in tents today because of their dispersion and intermarriages with Gentiles, but some Arabian tribes still live in tents and are able to preserve their traditional nomadic peculiarities.

These tents are held up by poles; the ends of each tent-cloth are drawn out by thick cords tied to long sturdy pins. These pins are driven as deeply as possible into the ground. Jael, Heber's wife, killed Sisera with such a tent pin (Judges 4:21).

Tents can be divided by camel- or goat-skin curtains into two or more rooms. They are usually made up of three spacious rooms. The entrance leads to the men's living room, which serves also as a bedroom. Women and children occupy the second room (Genesis 18:10). The third room is for the servants. However, if a man has more than one wife, as in the case of Jacob, the women may wish to live in separate tents (Genesis 31:33).

Arabs are very hospitable, and their tents are usually filled with friends and strangers. Arabs love to tell fables and proverbs, and to sit, as Abraham sat, in the entrance of their tent to be on the lookout for guests (Genesis 18:1). As the guest enters the tent, he will be greeted with a kiss. Then he removes his sandals and washes his hands and feet before sitting on a mat or rug. The moment he sits down, his head is anointed with olive oil as a sign of hospitality, and he is given water to drink. Water is a sign that the person is worthy of peaceful reception (Genesis 19:2).

Food

The diet consists mainly of homemade cheese and butter, milk, beef, mutton, game, and fowl (Genesis 18:7; I Kings 4:23; I Samuel 17:18; II Samuel 17:20; Proverbs 30:33). The women bake wheat and barley bread by rolling out the dough until it becomes thin. Then it is stuck on the side of the oven, where it bakes in a few seconds. This is similar to pizza-bread, but much more delicious (I Kings 19:6). They usually eat two meals a day—a light breakfast and a heavy dinner. Breakfast may be any time before noon. Bread and salt are signs of a covenant of peace between the host and the guest. The guest is made lord of the house, and his departure is delayed by requests to stay longer and eat more (Judges 19:5-10).

Camels

Many Semitic tribes still use camels for transportation. There are two types of camels—those with one hump (dromedary), and those with two humps (bactrian). Camels were created for desert travel. They are able to store more than nine gallons of water in their sack-cells, and they can scent water at a great distance. They are able to travel for about four weeks without food or water. They usually eat straw (teben), but when traveling, they eat any green things they may find on the way. Each of their feet has two long toes, resting upon hard elastic cushions, and their feet have very tough soles. This helps them endure extreme desert heat and keeps them from sinking into the sand. Camels are trained to kneel so that riders can mount them (Genesis 24:11).

Funerals

When death occurs, a wail is raised to announce the bad news. This "wail" is actually a sharp shriek, and is repeated until the people gather for the funeral. A handsome Arabian patchwork tent is erected during the funeral, and the men of the family receive condolences there for a few days after the burial. Separate tents are erected for the women, who give themselves up to unrestrained weeping. A "wailing woman" is employed at a large fee to keep the women occupied with grief for several hours. Then everyone is served bitter Arabian coffee before they depart.

Bargaining

Arabs love to bargain, whether they are rich or poor. The art of bargaining requires much time and energy and a shameless disregard for the truthfulness of the other party. During such interaction, some may shout, rebuke, and threaten with intensity. The atmosphere may appear to be charged with anger, yet this is the normal way some Arabs communicate. A wedding affords a very good example of the art of bargaining. Each family tries to bargain for the provision of a dowry, trousseau, furniture, housing, and other supplies. As the two families bargain for hours, sometimes for days, it is expected that one or both will reach a compromise with their gifts. It is the custom that an offer should be reduced at least 50 percent; and after looking piously surprised and horrified, they shake hands and accept the deal with thankful hearts and prayers for a long and prosperous life.

Desert Panorama

Arabs love nature, poetry, music, legends, and proverbs, and they enjoy the pleasures of life. This could be attributed to their easy nomadic existence and to the beauty of nature which surrounds them in a breathtaking panorama. The tall palm trees seem to rise up into the blue sky. The riders sway slowly on their camels, while the children herd sheep and goats. Veiled women move gracefully under the heavy earthen pots poised on their heads. The spell of the crystal purity of the desert air is captivating. The pungency of the cooking with onion and garlic makes eating a special pleasure, and the fragrance of incense and perfumes is delightful.

Weddings

Women are trained to serve their husbands and children, and the father is the supreme ruler of the household. This authority is handed down to the oldest son. Children are trained to honor their parents and to defend their family name. Parents select brides for their sons and spend much money on sumptuous weddings by slaughtering several lambs. These lambs are roasted whole, and many tables are filled with various appetizers. Arabian weddings are invariably as lavish and costly as the groom's family can afford. In order to entertain the guests, beautiful horses are trained to dance to music with precise rhythm and, along with their riders, are dressed in attractive costumes. Arabs have an obsession and a national passion for hospitality. It is one of their many unique characteristics that give Arabs the blessing of a coveted lifestyle.

The marriage of cousins among Arabs is very common, especially if there is a fortune to be kept in the family. This tradition is not restricted to Arabs, but is practiced by some Jews and Gentiles alike. However, these and other biblical traditions are crumbling under the pressure of Western standards and the pull of modern technology and materialism. Nowadays some Arabian women are veiled in primrose pink by dawn; during the rest of the day until the setting of the sun, they are veiled in violet, red, green, or gray. It appears that materialism and the pressures of modernization are affecting even the traditional Arabs. The Kur'an allows a man as many as four wives; the prophet Muhammed set the example by marrying nine women from various walks of life, one of them a Coptic Christian. It is said that the prophet married these women in order to convert them to Islam. Muslim men are allowed to marry outside their religion, but Muslim women are not. The logic for this is that men, as the head of the family, have a better chance to proselytize. Arabs have inherited this and other traditions, such as the multiplication and veiling of wives, from the Old Testament (Genesis 24:65, 29:15-30).

Arab Writers

Arabs from the many various tribes and lineages have covered the whole Middle East. The contributions of these people to world civilization is great indeed, in both the Orient and the West.

The following writers show merely the tip of the iceberg, so to speak, of Arabian culture:

Ibn Batuta (1304−1378) wrote widely on Islamic cultural and social history, and was one of the most renowned medieval travelers and geographers.

Al-Khowarizmi was born in 820 in Baghdad, and his very name gives us the mathematical term algorithm, a method for solving particular mathematical problems. Much of the mathematical knowledge of medieval Europe came from his work. The word *algebra* also is reputed to have been given to us by him.

Ibn al-Haytham (965−1040) was also a great mathematician.

He concocted an early work in optics, indicating that light rays emanate in straight lines in all directions from every point on a luminous surface. His work influenced Kepler and René Descartes.

Ibn Khaldûn (1332–1406) was considered the greatest Arabian historian. Born in Tunis, he later served his country as ambassador of the Moorish king to the court of Peter the Cruel in Castille, Spain. He also developed a consistent philosophy of history, as well as a unique method of writing in the areas of sociology and political economy. He sailed to Cairo in 1382, where he wrote extensively. Ibn Khaldûn was a charismatic diplomat. He stated that "man's distinguishing characteristic is the ability to think . . . and through thinking to cooperate." This is characteristic of Arabs: They love to cooperate with friends, but they become adamant when provoked to wrath.

Al-Farabi (d. 950) introduced Aristotelian logic to Islam and was also a master musician. It is said that he played the oud, an ancestor of the guitar, like a magician. While playing at a large gathering, he first made the people laugh, then made them cry, and finally put them to sleep.

Al-Kindi (d. 873) was a ninth-century philosopher who interpreted and introduced the writings of Plato and Aristotle to Europe. He produced more than 250 treatises, including dissertations on the nature of human reason, a topic perennially relevant to man. He was also well known to medical doctors and scientists of the Middle Ages, since he wrote on medicine, physics, psychology, and other important topics.

Ibn-Rushd (1126–1198) was better known as Averroes. An Arabian philospher living in Cordoba, Spain, he greatly influenced Jewish and Christian thought. He declared that philosophy was the highest form of inquiry, and that truth is derived from reason, not from faith. He wrote commentaries on Aristotle and attempted to delineate the tasks appropriate to faith and reason, pointing out that they were not in conflict. Thomas Aquinas, the great medieval Christian theologian, respected Averroes, who was also a lawyer and physician.

Al-Ghazali (1059–1111) was born near Baghdad, but lived in

Syria. He was a philosopher and a noted theologian. He wrote a beautiful version of the beatific vision, in which the individual could attain mystical unity with God. Like other intellectuals, he was well known in Europe, by the name Algazel.

Human culture would indeed be poorer in the absence of these and other descendants of Joktan, Ishmael, and Keturah. They gave the world many great philosophers whose mode of thought was determined primarily by their religious conditioning. Arab thought and culture became well known and influential in Europe and in the West, partly because Muslim philosophers translated many works of the Greeks, but also because they contributed other works of their own genius. Their writings were truly encyclopedic, comprising almost the whole edifice of knowledge.

Who are Today's Arabs?

The people called Arabs today can be defined primarily by a culture, not by geographical area or genealogy. Today's Arabs share a kindred way of life and a transmittable community of action, thought, belief, and feeling. The way they bring up their children, their family patterns, their social relations, and their love of nature show underlying similarities. It is important to note that they communicate through one medium of thought—the Arabic language. They cherish comparable traditions, customs, and history, and are enriched by much the same cultural heritage. Furthermore, they claim to have one symbolic system with which they relate to the world, a system that is derived primarily from Muslim tradition. The Arabs have a homogeneous ethnic heritage and a uniform civilization, common traditions of a glorious past, and a vital humanist participation in poetry, music, religion, songs, and legends. The Arabs of today receive great satisfaction from living vicariously in the glory and tradition of their great past.

The unifying power of Islam is derived from the Kur'an, Islam's sacred book, which has saved the Arabic language from disintegrating into a variety of local dialects. In this sense, the Kur'an has preserved the unity of thought and expression. Therefore Islam belongs to all whose native tongue is Arabic and who are associated with the same cultural background.

The people called Arabs today are descendants of several related racial stocks of the Mediterranean. Hence they are the inhabitants of Egypt, Iraq, Jordan, Syria, Lebanon, the Arabian Peninsula, the Persian Gulf states, the Sudan, Palestine, and North Africa, and their offspring living abroad.

Christian Arabs

An old man stands tied to a pole, patiently awaiting death by burning. He looked up toward heaven as the flames began to form an arc around his body, but to everyone's amazement, he does not burn. In desperation, a Roman executioner stabs him with a dagger, and the old man dies.

Polycarp, a disciple of John the Beloved and a bishop of the church at Smyrna, was martyred around the year 155 for his uncompromising faith in Jesus Christ. His great confession and prayer before his death remain as a rich heritage and encouragement for believers of all time. In his confession, he said, "Fourscore and six years have I been his servant, and he hath done me no wrong. How then can I blaspheme my King who saved me?" Before dying, he prayed, "Lord God Almighty, the Father of Thy beloved and blessed Son Jesus Christ, through whom we have received the knowledge of Thee; I bless Thee for that Thou hast granted me this day and hour, that I might receive a portion amongst the number of martyrs in the cup of Christ unto resurrection of eternal life."

With martyrs and church fathers like Polycarp, Christianity had an auspicious beginning in Asia Minor and other Arab-dominated areas. Roman Catholic and Eastern Orthodox churches continue to exist in the Arab world, having several million adherents. Arab churches are divided into Latin-rite Roman Catholic and Uniate—Eastern churches which have reunited with Rome, including Coptic Catholic, Syrian Catholic, Chaldean Catholic, and Maronite. The other Catholic group includes Eastern Orthodox churches such as Coptic,

Jacobite, and Nestorian. A brief review of history will help shed some light on the doctrinal errors under which many Arabs in these churches presently worship.

Historical research indicates that the ancient pagan religious system began with Nimrod, the son of Cush (Genesis 10:8), and his beautiful wife Queen Semiramis. The center of this religious system was Babylon, Nimrod's kingdom. The Bible teaches that Babylon represents a counterfeit, or imitation, of the true worship of the one and only living God (Genesis 11:3). The people did not build their city and tower with real and natural stone, but with brick and slime. The Lord Jesus told a parable concerning this very thing. He warned against idol worship and encouraged everyone to build his life upon the real Stone, or Rock, Christ Jesus (Matthew 7:24-27, 21:42; Revelation 9:20).

Nimrod became a builder of cities and a subjugator of people, and as such, false worship began to cling to him and his queen. Through a series of complex changes, Nimrod was worshiped as the husband of Semiramis, and later on, as her son. It was this latter form of worship that captured the allegiance of the ancient world. The divinity of the son passed to the mother, and both were worshiped as mother and child.

The mother became the queen of heaven, the same queen of heaven whom God pointed out to Jeremiah. The Israelites were guilty of making cakes as an offering to her (Jeremiah 7:18). This same tradition appears in the Easter cakes made by women in various Orthodox churches. In ancient times, perhaps fifteen hundred years before Christ, sacred bread was used by the Chaldeans in the adoration of the queen of heaven. Our modern word *bun* comes from the root word *boun,* which means *bread.* In warning against worshiping Mary, Saint Epiphanus (310−403) noted that some women in Thrace, Scythia, Greece, and Arabia were adoring the Virgin as a goddess and offering a type of cake to her.

The husband-son of the queen was known as Tammuz and was said to have undergone a death and resurrection. The annual commemoration of this event was preceded by a forty-day fast and accompanied by weeping and rejoicing. The worship of this Tammuz is hated by God. In Ezekiel 8:3, 14, the Jewish women of Jerusalem committed abomination by weeping for Tammuz, who had become an idol, a false Christ, and this provoked God to wrath. Tammuz was also the husband-brother of Ishtar, the Babylonian goddess of fertility. The word Easter came from Ishtar, whom the Ephesians worshiped as "the great goddess Diana" (Acts 19:23-35). Easter denotes fertility, not resurrection. Only believers in Jesus Christ will have resurrection (I Corinthians 15:20-23). Fertility is earthly and temporary, but resurrection is heavenly and eternal.

The worship of this mother-child pair spread throughout the ancient world. In Babylon they were known as Rhea and Tammuz; in Egypt, Isis and Osiris; in India, Isi and Iswara; in Asia, Cybele and Deoius; in Rome, Venus and Jupiter-puer; in Greece, Ceres and Plutus. This universal religious worship is still with us today when the mother of Jesus is divinized, at times, made to surpass him in greatness.

This is exactly what has happened in Catholic and Orthodox churches, to the extent that the authority of Scripture alone has been downplayed. As far back as the Nicene Council (325 A.D.), the representatives of the Egyptian church held that the three persons of the Trinity were the Father, the Virgin Mary, and their Son. The pagan tendency for the mother to be divinized is obvious.

The cult of Mary began in the Eastern churches, but later developed in the Roman churches also. The elevation of the Virgin was actually a result of early doctrinal disputes concerning the nature of Christ. The Virgin birth was consistently appealed to as proof of the reality of Jesus' two natures (God-man), and the unity of his person (one Lord), However, John of Damascus, an early Eastern father, said, "Mary is the sovereign Lady to whom the whole creation is made subject by her Son."

The title of mediatrix has also been applied to Mary by both Eastern and Roman churches, by Saint Andrew of Crete in the East in the 700s, and by Saint Bernard in the West in the

1100s. There are at least three senses in which Mary is said to mediate. Jesus came to man through her, and in that sense she mediated between God and man. Second, it is said that Mary mediates the gifts to men from heaven. According to Pope Leo XIII: "In this light, Mary is mediatrix, not only as one through whom the divine gift is transmitted to men, but also as the one who, in the name of mankind, responds to the divine initiative." Third, Mary, in her intense suffering, mediated at the crucifixion with Christ and, in this sense, would be a co-redeemer.

Pius X, Pius XII, Benedict XV—all consider Mary co-redeemer. Pius X said of her, "Jesus with Mary was to crush the serpent's head at the Incarnation, the Word assuming Flesh through Mary and chiefly at the Passion when Jesus dying for mankind, Mary was joined to Him by a 'union of will and suffering.'" Benedict XV, in *Inter Sodalicia*, states, "Insofar as it was hers to do . . . she may justly be said to have redeemed together with Christ the human race." A logical concomitant of the doctrine of coredemption is that Mary, also, was sinless. Pope Pius IX made the Immaculate Conception a doctrine of the church—that there was no sin nature in Mary from the moment she was conceived by her mother. On the other hand, the Bible says that "all have sinned" (Romans 3:23, 5:12; Galatians 3:22).

This doctrinal development leads to denials of Scripture by the Roman Catholic and Eastern Orthodox churches. "For there is one God, and one mediator between God and men, the man Christ Jesus" (I Timothy 2:5). This is denied by the doctrine of Mary, mediatrix. "Neither is there salvation in any other: for there is none other name under heaven given among men, whereby we must be saved" (Acts 4:12). This is denied by the doctrine of Mary, co-redemptrix.

The doctrine of purgatory is another ancient dogma grafted onto the teaching of the Bible. The greatest of the Greek philosophers, Plato, was a proponent of this doctrine. He taught that the dead must endure their deserved punishment for a time before they pass to a more comfortable celestial habitation. The noted Roman poet Virgil gave some literary expression to this doctrine, and Dante styled his *Inferno* after the pattern of Virgil. The grafting of such a doctrine into Christendom leads to a further denial of Scripture. The Bible says, "And as it is appointed unto men once to die, but after this the judgment" (Hebrews 9:27).

Christian Arabs in both western and eastern churches are living under these denials of Scripture. The Coptic church and the Syrian and Chaldean churches hold further problematical positions. The Coptic church is famous for its early monastic movement, and also for its adherence to a theological position known as monophysitism, meaning *one nature*. In the 400s, a Coptic father, Eutyches, held that after the Incarnation, Christ had only one nature, the divine. So the divinity of Christ was emphasized, but the Incarnation was effectively denied, since there was no human nature involved. The truly human Christ became so deified that his humanity and unique person were overlooked.

The Chaldean and Syrian churches, also known as Nestorian, have taken another tack. Nestorius, who became Patriarch of Constantinople in 428, held that Jesus was a man who became one with God by a moral union, that Jesus was not "the Word made flesh" (John 1:14). The difference is very subtle, but most important. If one man became God, then the way could be open for other men to become God. The emphasis here is on man being active and doing something to become God. This has been the dream of sinful man since the time of Adam. The orthodox position (not to be confused with the Orthodox church) has been that the human and divine natures of Christ are in true union, or, as the Council of Chalcedon (451) states it, "in two natures, without confusion, without change, without division, without separation; the distinction of natures being in no way annulled by the union, but rather the characteristics of each nature being preserved and coming together to form one person and subsistence, not as parted or separated into two persons, but one and the same Son and Only-begotten God the Word, Lord Jesus Christ."

However, eastern churches have not been able to get away from the influence of Nestorius. These doctrinal errors lead to further tendencies to depart from the faith.

The Maronites are good examples of a very old and well-established body of Christian Arabs. They are of Syrian origin, and their patron saint is John Maroun, who lived in a monastery near Antioch, that famous town where the disciples were first called Christians (Acts 11:26). Tradition asserts that Mar (Saint) Nikhoula, patron of the Roum-Orthodox, plucked out the eye of Maroun in a quarrel. As a result of this predicament, Mar Maroun instructed his followers to detach themselves from the Syrian Orthodox church and form their own hierarchy. Later on, the Orthodox church began to harass them, and the Maronites fled Syria and took refuge in the deep valleys of northern Lebanon near Quadisha. They gradually moved to southern Lebanon and wisely formed an alliance with the Druze, who were prominent landowners and respected patriots. After World War I and the coming of French mandate rule, the Maronites gained favor with the Catholic French and enough political power to achieve a constitutional mandate that the president of Lebanon be from the minority Maronite sect. This kind of diplomatic maneuvering has continued to generate political tensions in the Middle East, especially in Lebanon.

The Maronites pride themselves on their economic, political and cultural ties to the United States and Europe. This feeling of superiority is a distinctive mark which makes them different from the Lebanese Islamic majority; therefore, they have good reason to feel insecure. Because of this, they have developed clan loyalties like those of Ireland and Scotland which believe that violence is as much a source for salvation and self-preservation as the cross. The Maronites number about 500,000 and have dominated Lebanese politics for more than four decades, ruling over a population of about 3.5 million. Hence their fear of being swallowed up and ostracized by the Muslim majority in Lebanon continues to give them the impetus to resort to violence in order to protect their political power.

Today, about 7.36 percent of the Arab population of the world is affiliated with various Christian groups. Combinations of Orthodox and Roman Catholic groups make a significant total in various Middle Eastern countries. Egypt has over 7 million Orthodox (Coptic) and Catholic Arabs, and Lebanon, more than one million. In Syria there are about 724,000 Orthodox and Catholic Arabs, around 92,000 in Jordan, and the rest are scattered in many parts of the world.

The Druze Arabs

On the mountain of Carmel overlooking the Mediterranean, at the outskirts of the village of Usfiya, Israel, the majority of some 60,000 Druze citizens live. In Arabia, Mount Carmel is known as El-Mahrakah, which means *the burning*, or *the sacrifice*. This is where Elijah brought fire from heaven on the sacrifice, destroying all 450 prophets of Baal (I Kings 18:20-40). The Druze Arabs living around this historical site practice an annual sacrifice at the Mount. Not far from Mt. Carmel flows the Kishon—in Arabic, Nahr El-Mukatta, *the river of slaughter.* Nearby is Tell Kasis, *the hill of the priest.* Also near is a perennial well of water that was used to soak the altar and fill the trenches around it. This water is said to flow even in the midst of drought.

Israel provides a home for the smallest Druze community in the Middle East, dwarfed by some million of their brethren living in Lebanon, Syria, and elsewhere. The degree of their integration into surrounding communities differs from country to country. Israel's Druze are granted a high degree of autonomy in their domestic affairs, mainly because they serve with the Israeli armed forces. The Druze are loyal to friends and have always identified themselves with the strongest force around them. Their current alignment with Israel is in concert with their historical character. For instance, they supported the Ottoman Turks in the fifteenth century against Egypt. They supported the French in Syria. Moreover, when Israel became a nation in 1948, many Syrian Druze families moved there, the men joining their brethren in the Israeli armed forces. An old

Druze patriarch once said to me, "In my opinion, whoever is in power and gives us security and equality, he should get our loyal support." It is interesting to note that the Druze religion consider Jethro to be greater than Moses, because God was reincarnated in his person, as well as in the person of Pythagoras, Alexander the Great, king David, and many others.

The Druze religion is a mystical offshoot of the Shiite sect of Islam, dating back to the eleventh century. The Shiite sect was founded by the Fatimid Caliph, al-Hakim bi-amr Allah, who ruled in Cairo from 996 through 1021 A.D. and proclaimed himself the reincarnation of God. The Druze believe he really is the incarnation of God and that he is still living, but hidden until his time shall come.

These enigmatic people are an offshoot of Islam, as previously mentioned. However, they are neither Muslim nor Christian, nor do they adhere to any religion other than their own. They have their roots in a splinter group from the Ismaili branch of Islam, which founded the Fatimid Caliphate of Egypt in the tenth century. The Druze are erroneously named after Nashtakeen al-Darazi, a missionary who set out to convert the Muslim and Christian peoples to his new faith. The Druze like to be called Muwahedeen, meaning that they worship only one God. Life for them is eternal through a continuous cycle of death and rebirth, reincarnation. Souls neither die nor sleep, but continue to develop until their full potential is reached, at which time they unite with the universal mind (God). There is no hell; the only penalty is the soul's regret at not having reached the goals and heights of perfection and purity. Druze soldiers are extremely brave, knowing that upon death they will immediately inherit a younger, stronger body and will have another chance to work toward perfection, to attain more noble goals. No wonder their soldiers are valiant and fierce on the battlefield! Since the Druze believe in reincarnation and the possibility of attaining perfection by works, there is no need for a redeemer. These doctrinal obstacles, as well as their close family and community life, make evangelism among this group of Arabs most difficult.

The Druze of Lebanon have seen their fortunes rise and fall throughout the past millennium. The Turkish Sultans collaborated with the disciplined warlike Druze leaders and gave them freedom to practice their own autonomy in the Shouf mountains, trusting them to exercise control over the Christians and Muslims living in their area. During the sixteenth and early seventeenth centuries, the Druze were prominent landowners and played an important role in the politics of Lebanon and Syria. They were given a miniempire by the Turks, extending from the Shouf mountains to Beirut and Sidon in Lebanon, and to Tripoli and Latakia in Syria. However, in the 1850s, inter-religious hostility between the Christians and Druze mounted to a point that massacres were carried out by one community against the other. This led to civil war and the intervention of the European Christian nations in support of the Christians in Lebanon. Thereafter, a Christian military governor assumed authority over Lebanon, and large numbers of the Druze departed in fear of Christian reprisals, moving eastward to the Houran mountains of Syria. There they established a stronghold and to this day, their largest concentration remains there. Because of Syria's hospitality, the Druze constitute a loyal and hard-working minority there, as they do in Israel.

When the French defeated the Turkish empire and seized Lebanon in 1918, new turmoil broke out in Lebanon and Syria. Instead of giving the people a self-rule policy, France, a Catholic nation, favored the Christian Maronites in Lebanon. However, under the leadership of the Druze Sultan Pasha al-Attrash of Syria, a successful rebellion was mounted in 1925 against the French in both Lebanon and Syria. For a time it appeared that France would allow the people to determine their own destiny, but history teaches that all conquerors are alike. France prevailed against the Druze and exerted central control over them in Syria and Lebanon, permitting them to have dominion only over their local communities and internal affairs.

When Lebanon became independent from France in 1943,

its newly adopted constitution required that the nation's president must be a Maronite Christian, and the Druze were left out of key positions. French intervention in Lebanon from 1918 until 1943 had given a continued impetus to the Maronite Catholics. The Druze continue to live in the Shouf mountains and defend their territory and human rights vigorously.

Because the Druze tend to conceal the tenets of their inscrutable faith, secrecy and security are the hallmark of their religion. Consequently, they feign adherence to Christianity, Judaism, or Islam when there is danger of persecution and discrimination. However, they always have been known as fearless and skillful fighters. Their defiance of the Lebanese army and the American fleet, in the recent civil war in Lebanon, attests to this very fact. The Druze put much emphasis on honor, prestige, and family ties. When a member of the family is in trouble, the whole family is obligated to support the individual, in relation to the degree of kinship—the close relative is favored over the more distant one. One Arab proverb says, "I will help my brother against my cousin, and I will help my cousin against the stranger."

Islam

The scene is Al-Azhar in Cairo, Egypt, the greatest of Islamic universities for more than one thousand years. The courtyard is filled with the sound of rhythmic Kur'anic quotations chanted by students. Calloused knees are on prayer mats and heads bob in unison as entire books of the Kur'an are repeated without a mistake. The garments of this academic religious community consist of loose, flowing robes, with satin petticoats for the rich. The poor wear long buttoned robes without petticoats. After eight to twelve years of residence, the student becomes a sheikh, with one burning purpose—to further the course of Islam. This community exists around the Kur'an, which has exerted a continuous and unifying influence on Arab culture and life. All Muslims are commanded by Muhammed to study the Kur'an in Arabic. In this sense, the book has brought unified language and a strong Arabic identity to Christians and Druze, as well as to Muslims and other Arabs.

With the rise of Islam, the course of history in the Middle Ages was radically changed. The Greco-Roman domination in politics and culture was ended, and a new religion with a new way of life were introduced. Arabic became the *lingua franca*, and a new way of thought was inaugurated. The establishment of this new order can be viewed as the end of ancient times for the Middle East, the beginning of the Middle Ages. Unlike medieval Europe, the Muslim Middle Ages were characterized by splendor, glory, and empire.

This great change began at the caravan stop of Mecca, through the prophet of Islam, Muhammed, born in 570 into the tribe of Quraysh, the keepers of the sacred Kaaba. The Kaaba is the holiest place in Islam, yet it existed centuries before the time of Muhammed. According to Muslim tradition, Abraham and Ishmael built the Kaaba, a roughly cubical structure fifty feet high, as a replica of God's house in heaven. In the corner is the sacred black stone which Gabriel brought to Abraham from paradise.

Mecca owed its existence to a well, Zamzam, identified by Muslims as the well from which Hagar and Ishmael drank while in the wilderness (Genesis 21:19). Muhammed lived in this settlement and in the atmosphere of the Kaaba. No one really knows the name he was given at birth. Muhammed means *most highly praised.*

At age twenty-five, Muhammed married a wealthy widow, Khadija, a successful business woman fifteen years his senior, from the same tribe of Quraysh. Through her, Muhammed obtained the economic security to pursue a free life of contemplation and meditation. He often visited an isolated cave on a barren hill outside Mecca, and it was there in 610 A.D. that he received his first revelation in the form of the reverberation of a bell. Later he identified this as the voice of the angel Gabriel. The call was purely auditory and had no visual aspects as was the case with Moses, Paul, and Isaiah. Muhammed was bidden by the angel to begin reciting the Kur'an. Since Muhammed could neither read nor write, his recitation of the Kur'an in perfect Arabic is cited as miraculous.

Muhammed gradually broke away from Judaism and Christianity. He replaced the Sabbath with Friday, substituted the muezzin's call to prayer for the sound of church bells, and changed the direction of kneeling for prayers from Jerusalem to Mecca. Muhammed also cleansed the Kaaba personally. He destroyed hundreds of idols, declaring, "Truth hath come and falsehood hath vanished." In 630 he sanctioned a pilgrimage to the Kaaba for all physically able Muslims and declared the area around it *haram*, or *forbidden*, to non-Muslims.

In the month of al-Hijjah, this pilgrimage still takes place, and the population of Mecca swells by hundreds of thousands. Every able Muslim is required to visit Mecca at least once in a lifetime. When the ceremonies in Mecca begin, the pilgrims walk around the Kaaba seven times, kiss the black stone, smoothed from millions of hands and lips, and drink from the well Zamzam. Then they move toward Mount Arafat, passing through the valley of Mina, identified as the place where Abraham left Hagar and Ishmael. While in Mina, the pilgrims cast seven stones, three times, in commemoration of Abraham's stoning of Satan, who appeared to him there. The ceremony ends with the sacrifice of a camel, sheep, or goat in remembrance of Ishmael, rather than of Isaac, who was taken up the mount by Abraham to be sacrificed. This is the greatest festival in the Muslim calendar. After the ceremony rituals, the pilgrims are sanctified and may proudly be called *hajj*, or holy men.

Beginning as a tiny religious community in Saudi Arabia, today Islam embraces more than one billion people of all colors and races, forming a solid block from Morocco to Pakistan and claiming numerous millions in India, Indonesia, Russia, and many other parts of the world. Islam has no priesthood or sacraments. It was meant to be a religious brotherhood in which the bonds of Islam would take the place of the bonds of tribal kinship.

The Kur'an and the five pillars of Islam are the heart of the faith. The Kur'an is God's final revelation to man and supersedes all earlier ones. Muhammed is the "seal of the prophets," the last and greatest in a line of twenty-eight, stretching from Adam through Noah, Abraham, Moses, and Jesus. Muslims claim that the Comforter, or paraclete, promised by Jesus in John 16:7 has appeared in the person of Muhammed, who was chosen by God to give the Kur'an. He was also chosen to teach the doctrine of total *submission* to the will of God. This is the meaning of the word Islam in Arabic. Muhammed was called to destroy idolatry, to correct the adulterated message of God given to Jesus. (Muslims believe the Bible was adulterated by Paul and other sinful men). Muhammed was also called to replace the cross with a crescent, a symbol of political power.

Islam stresses the unity, majesty, and sovereignty of the one true Allah. Yet Allah is different from the God and Father of Jesus Christ. Allah is utterly remote and cannot be known in a personal way, nor can he be affected by man's rebellious Adamic nature. Therefore, Islam teaches that all sins are insignificant compared with the blasphemy of associating another deity with Allah. The height of sin, then, would be the belief that God should become incarnate. Thus there is no need for the atonement of sin, nor is it necessary to seek God's forgiveness on a moral foundation.

Submission is the norm for the Muslim. However, since Allah is remote, he cannot be submitted to personally; only his will as known in the Kur'an can be submitted to. Allah has chosen not to reveal his person, but only his will, as revealed through Muhammed.

The religious duties of a Muslim can be summarized under these five categories, the five pillars of Islam:

1. *Profession of Faith.* To believe in Allah is not enough. The Muslim must make a public oral profession: "There is no God but Allah, and Muhammed is the messenger of Allah".

2. *Prescribed Prayers.* Prayers must be offered five times a day—at dawn, midday, mid-afternoon, sunset, and two hours after sunset. Daniel followed a three-times-a-day practice, fac-

ing Jerusalem through opened windows (Daniel 6:10). Muslims pray facing Mecca. They are not ashamed of their God, and they shout his name from "upon the housetops" (Matthew 10:27). When praying, the Muslims are in a state of legal purity. Prayer follows an identical pattern of bodily postures; standing, sitting, and prostrate. During each of the five prayer-times, the opening chapter of the Kur'an, which has often been likened to the Lord's Prayer, is repeated four times. One is, of course, free to engage in individual prayer and supplication.

Congregational prayer takes place Friday at noon in the mosques, where a special area is reserved for veiled women worshipers. (In the Old Testament, veiling was a symbol of submission. See Genesis 24:65; cf. I Corinthians 11:5-7). The mosques have no pictures or pews. The walls are decorated with passages from the Kur'an and the names of the prophet. The worshipers usually arrange themselves in straight parallel rows and follow their leader (Imam) in their bodily postures and genuflexions. A prominent feature of the Friday service is the sermon delivered by the Imam from a pulpit. Both pulpit and sermon show Christian influence.

3. *Fasting.* Like Moses, Daniel, and Jesus, Muslims also fast. In Islam, fasting, except when voluntary, is restricted to the month of Ramadan, the month when the Kur'an was revealed. Abstinence from food, drink, smoking, and all desire of the flesh must be practiced during each day from dawn until sunset. In the Arabian Peninsula and Libya, this obligation is enforced by law. The Muslim calendar is based on twelve lunar months, and therefore it is approximately eleven days shorter than the solar year. In other words, Ramadan falls a bit earlier each year, and goes full cycle through the Gregorian (Western) calendar about every thirty-three years.

4. *Alms Giving.* Each Muslim is required to give alms to the poor, amounting to 2.5 percent, or one-fourtieth, of his income. For this reason, it is not uncommon to see beggars on the streets or around entrances to mosques in Muslim lands.

5. *Pilgrimage.* A visit to the holy city of Mecca is required of every able-bodied Muslim who can afford it, at least once in a lifetime.

The holy war, or *jihad,* could be called a sixth pillar. It is the duty of all healthy male Muslims to bear arms. Islam owes much of its expansion as a world religion to this tenet. Death in jihad is martyrdom and "the path of Allah," to secure the warrior paradise and special heavenly privileges. Arabic has a special word for jihad conquests—*fateh,* or *opening*—that is, they are openings for the path of Islam.

Islam is Christianity's greatest theological challenge. Islam's attitude is somewhat similar to that of Christianity toward Judaism. Christianity views the Old Testament as an incomplete revelation of God, fulfilled and completed by God's revelation in the New Testament. Islam maintains that the Kur'an supersedes and corrects all previous revelations of God.

A more radical critique by Islam is that the New Testament documents have been severely corrupted, particularly by Paul, so that the record we have is untrustworthy. It was for this reason that Muhammed was chosen by God to reveal the trustworthiness of the Kur'an.

Islam, then, denies the following Christian doctrines:

1. *The Trinity.* The doctrine of the Trinity is utterly abhorrent to Islam. In Islam's conception, the Trinity consists of God, the Virgin Mary, and their son, Jesus, who was produced by methods of human generation. However, the Kur'an teaches that Jesus was sent by God and encourages all Muslims to honor him.

2. *The Deity of Christ.* Jesus' deity is totally rejected by Islam because of the absolute oneness of God. The doctrine of incarnation is idolatrous and blasphemous to Islam.

3. *The Crucifixion of Christ.* The Kur'an teaches that Christ did not die on the cross, but that another, in his likeness, died: "Yet they [the Jews] did not slay him, neither crucified him, only a likeness of that was shown to them . . . and they slew

him not of a certainty—no indeed, God raised him up to himself; God is All-mighty, All-wise" (Women 4:157-58).

That quotation is contradictory, because the Kur'an also says, "When God said, 'Jesus, I will make thee die and will raise thee up to myself, and I will purify thee of those who believe not. I will set thy followers above the unbelievers till the resurrection day'" (House of Imran 3:55).

In another verse from the Kur'an, confirming the death and resurrection of Christ, Jesus said to the Jews, "Peace be upon me the day I was born, and the day I die, and the day I am raised up alive" (Mary 19:33). One more verse should be sufficient to prove that the Kur'an totally agrees with the gospel (Injeel). Jesus said to God, "I was a witness over them [the people] while I remained among them: but when thou made me die, thou was thyself the watcher over them" (Table 5:117).

4. *The Authenticity of the Bible.* Muslims claim that Paul and other Christians have added to the original manuscripts, deleting all Scriptures dealing with the coming of Muhammed as the seal of the prophets.

The moral standards and the disunity of Christendom are also abhorrent to Islam. Although the Muslim is permitted to divorce his wife for lesser reasons than adultery, there are fewer divorces in Islam than in Christianity. The Muslim looks with disdain at the Christian of low moral conduct and does not respond to or respect the gospel that is being proclaimed by the fragmented man-made denominations. Western idolization of Israel is another great offense to Islam and their counterparts.

Christians generally have failed to come to grips with these Kur'anic and Islamic denials, but have tried in vain to prove the truth of the gospel of Christ by comparing it with the Kur'an. This method is doomed to failure, because the Lord does not bless any method of evangelism other than that of the Bible. The gospel of Christ can be and must be proclaimed authentically *only* on the basis of the Bible, not as a hybrid of Kur'an and Bible.

Islam has been the only world religion to win great numbers of converts from Christendom. From the seventh century until recent times, Christianity has steadily lost ground to the aggressive and relentless drive of Islam. Countries that were once under the cross have taken up the crescent as their banner. Palestine, the home of Jesus and the Apostles, became a protectorate of the Arab Caliphs under Islam. Egypt, the center of theology from the time of Origen to Athanasius, came under the umbrella of Mecca. North Africa, where Augustine, Tertullian, Cyprian, and other great apologists and theologians defended the faith (Jude 3), was incorporated into the world of Islam. Asia Minor (modern Turkey) was a hotbed of early church activity. The seven churches of the Book of Revelation were in Turkey as well as the cities of Antioch, Troas, Lystra, and Tarsus. Renowned church Fathers such as Ignatius and Polycarp were from Turkey, an area now almost totally under strict Muslim domination. Basically four out of five early Christian cities were conquered and influenced by Islam*—Constantinople, Alexandria, Antioch, and Jerusalem. Only Rome was spared for a specific prophetic reason (Revelation 17:1-9)!

---

*The term 'Islam' has been used interchangeably in this book with the word 'Arab' mainly because Muhammed had commanded all the Muslims to study and recite the Kur'an in Arabic. However, the Arabs are approximately two hundred million peoples, but when the Muslims from the various countries of the world are added to the Arabs, their number reaches nearly one billion.

Chapter Three
God's Prophetic Clock

Israel in Retrospect

History attests to the fact that no nation has ever been despised and persecuted and uprooted as much as Israel. This hatred, bigotry, and dispersion faced by Jews is part of God's judgment upon them for their disbelief and rebellion. God said,

> When the house of Israel dwelt in their own land, they defiled it by their own way. . . . Wherefore I poured my fury upon them for the blood that they had shed upon the land, and for their idols. . . . And I scattered them among the heathen, and they were dispersed through the countries (Ezekiel 36:17-19).

God chose the Jews for a prophetic reason, but because they continually disobeyed him, he pronounced judgment upon them: "For the punishment of the iniquity . . . of my people is greater than the punishment of the sin of Sodom" (Lamentations 4:6).

For example, the indelible scar of a chronic series of persecutions by "Christian" Crusaders has been ingrained in the Jewish memory. It is said that the Crusaders bathed the Promised Land with Jewish blood. Pregnant women, children, and old folks were butchered; the young were massacred, some were burned alive. It is so ironic that all this was done in the name of Christ and under the sign of the cross.

During the Inquisition (15th and 16th centuries), the European "Christians" tortured and burned to death millions of Jews. During the latter part of the last century, thousands of Jews were brutally beaten and persecuted in Russia and the Ukraine, Poland, Rumania, and in other parts of eastern Europe. Such violent attacks more often than not were carried out by "Christians" at Christmas or Easter—all in the name of Christ and under the sign of the cross. I do not really believe that any truly born-again Christians could have been among those demonized men. But the Jews have survived and out-lived all their conquerors.

At this time, I would like to point out a fact often overlooked by many historians—that Islam has shown more compassion toward the Jews than has Christendom. There has never been an Islamic equivalent of the Catholic Inquisition or the Holo-caust of Hitler's regime. It is true that Islam was often spread by the sword and caused many Jews to flee into Russia and eastern Europe, but Islamic persecution of the Jews had never reached the horror and savagery of that of Christendom. In fact, Islamic countries have opened their doors to Jewish refu-gees fleeing from faraway places. Jewish scholars were able to attain high positions in the Arab world and enjoy the un-matched hospitality of their blood relatives, the Arabs.

In the same vein, the Kur'an recognizes the fact that God chose Jewish prophets in the Old and New Testaments to reveal his will. The Kur'an also agrees with the Bible that the Jewish rulers and religious leaders persecuted God's prophets and crucified the Lord Jesus. Moreover, the Kur'an reveres God's prophets of both Testaments and declares the Jewish nation to be guilty of their innocent blood:

> We gave to Moses the Book—and we gave Jesus son of Mary the clear signs, and confirmed him with the Holy Spirit, and whensoever there come to you a Messenger with that your souls had not desired, did you become arrogant, and some cry lies [to Moses and Old Testament prophets], and some slay

[Christ and New Testament prophets] (Cow 2:87; cf. Acts 7:52; I Thessalonians 2:14-16).

Conversely, it pleased the Lord to single out a most stiff-necked people (Deuteronomy 9:6), in order that he might fulfill his immutable prophetic plan. No other nation has witnessed God's presence as have the Jews. The history of Israel is a steady progression of unusual miracles. God chose the Jews to be his witnesses (Isaiah 43:10). They saw God in action as he parted the Red Sea and the Jordan River, so that they could enter the land safely on dry ground. The walls of Jericho crumbled and fell at the sound of trumpets, and the sun stood still for nearly a day as the Jews watched with awe the defeat of their enemies (Joshua 10:12-14). God led them in the wilderness by a pillar of cloud by day and by a pillar of fire by night. God fed them and took care of all their needs for forty years in the wilderness, and throughout the centuries they have been miraculously preserved for a future prophetic reason.

Zionism

Zionism is nothing more than the burning desire of the Jews to return to Zion, the Promised Land (Psalm 137:1-4; Jeremiah 23:8). Zionism is linked with the feverish hope of national restoration as a result of the coming Messiah. However, Rabbi Kalisher, a nineteenth-century Prussian Jew, argued that the Jews need not wait for the return of the Messiah before going back to the Promised Land. Similar views were later expressed by Moses Hess, a German Marxist who, in his book *Rome and Jerusalem*, called for a national emancipation movement among Jews. Likewise, in the West and Europe, ideas of this kind began to take root. As mass persecutions gradually increased, many orthodox and self-confessed agnostic Jews left for Palestine. The Middle East was occupied at that time by the Turks.

Moreover, an Austrian journalist by the name of Theodore Herzl contributed much to the prophetic cause of Zionism. He was not aware that God was using him, along with others, to fulfill prophecy. Nevertheless, Herzl went to Paris in 1896 to report the Dreyfus Case for a Viennese newspaper. The Dreyfus Case occupied Europe for a long time because of its controversial nature.

Dreyfus, a Jew, was a respected high-ranking officer in the French army. Due to anti-Semitic sentiments existing in Europe during that time, Dreyfus was used as a scapegoat and falsely accused of collaborating with the Germans. He was finally sentenced to lifelong exile, in spite of the fact that there was no incriminating evidence.

The Dreyfus Case, coupled with Herzl's disenchantment with anti-Semitism, gave him the impetus to write *Der Judenstaat* (*The Jewish State*). In 1897, he organized and presided over the first Zionist congress in Basel, Switzerland. He was convinced that political Zionism was the only practical answer to the chronic problem of anti-Semitism. Soon this newly formed organization was desperately seeking to establish a national home for the uprooted Jewish people. Uganda was considered as a possible location, but only Palestine would fulfill prophecy.

The philosopher Martin Buber and his counterparts had in mind a Jewish settlement in Palestine that would follow the Messianic moral code. Rather than developing a distinctly Jewish state, they were willing to coexist and cooperate with the local Arabs in order to secure peace for all concerned. Some Zionists thought Buber's views unrealistic, while others maintained they were too idealistic. Much debate and deliberation ensued.

At the turn of the twentieth century, neither the Arabs nor the European Zionists were belligerent toward each other. However, the Allies (the British and the French) had adopted pro-Jewish attitudes as a result of Christian-Zionist theological persuasion from evangelical circles during the nineteenth century. The Allies decided it was to their advantage politically and economically to exploit this historical event of the Jews return to Palestine. They were aware of the fact that the Turks had outlived their usefulness in the Middle East. After all, the Allies had wanted to end the Turkish subjugation of the Arabs since 1516—especially now, since the Turks were allied with Germany and Austria during World War I.

With the help of Lawrence of Arabia, a British agent serving in the Middle East, the Allies were able to woo key Arab leaders and persuade them to fight against the Turks in order to uproot them from their lands. In return, the British made some promises they did not intend to keep. They promised Emir Faisal I (who became king of Iraq in 1920) a postwar independent Arab state. Those promises were made to Sherif Hussein of Mecca by Sir Henry McMahon, the British High Commissioner in Egypt.

In 1917, the British also made promises to the Zionist organization, to the effect that Palestine would become an independent Jewish national home. This was known as the Balfour Declaration, the famous letter from Lord Balfour sent to the British Zionist chemist, Chaim Weizmann. This kind of subtle political maneuvering overturned Martin Buber's idea of peaceful coexistence between Arabs and Jews and set the Middle East on a course of hostility and bloody wars. I believe, along with many others, that the conflict between Arabs and Jews has already reached a point of no return.

The period from 1922 through 1947 was filled with sporadic turmoil. Arabs and Jews led many bloody assaults on opposite villages, forcing the other to retaliate with vengeance. This protracted violence led the United Nations, in 1947, to vote for the "partition plan," dividing Palestine between the Arabs and the Jews, with Jerusalem under U.N. control. The Jews welcomed the decision, and a year later the world witnessed with amazement the rebirth of the physical Israel. These historical events were allowed to be fulfilled by God's sovereign prophetic plan.

According to my understanding of the Bible, God exercises his sovereign will in four different ways. First, God has a perfect will and encourages his servants to become perfect (Genesis 17:1; Matthew 5:48). I believe God is speaking here of spiritual maturity, not of perfection. Since the posterity of Adam is totally depraved (the human nature being polluted with sin), no one can attain perfection. The Lord Jesus is the only perfect One, because he is impeccable (he cannot sin nor was he able to sin). The impeccability of Christ has been a controversial topic among evangelical Christians and theologians.

Second, God has a preceptive will and exhorts his people to put their biblical knowledge into practice and to engage in fellowship with him through daily Bible study and meditation. Only then does God give prosperity and success to those who diligently seek him (Joshua 1:8; Psalm 1:1-3). This refers to spiritual prosperity and success, not necessarily financial.

Third, since we have inherited the Adamic sin-nature by imputation (Adam's sin was credited to mankind by transferral), the human race is behaving according to God's permissive will. God gave man the freedom of choice and holds him accountable according to his good or evil deeds. And of course, man is held accountable for his volitional response also to the free gift of salvation through faith in Christ Jesus (John 8:24, 36).

Finally, God has a prophetic will that nothing can alter nor hinder. God uses everything and everyone he has created to accomplish his sovereign prophetic will (Isaiah 46:9-11, 55:11; Revelation 17:17). History is the scenario that God has written, and the whole world participates involuntarily in this drama.

THE PROMISED LAND

The Origin of Canaan

The origin of Canaan is recorded in Genesis 10:6: "And the sons of Ham; Cush, and Mizraim, and Phut, and Canaan." All the direct descendants of Canaan are listed in the same chapter:

> And Canaan begat Sidon his firstborn, and Heth, and
> the Jebusite, and the Amorite, and the Girgasite, and

the Hivite, and the Arkite, and the Sinite, and the Arvadite, and the Zemarite, and the Hamathite: and afterward were the families of the Canaanites spread abroad (Genesis 10:15-18).

The identity of Canaan and his descendants seems quite clear from the above Scripture references. However, when other references are compared, there is an apparent problem. When Genesis 15:21 is reviewed, the Amorites and Canaanites seem to be two different peoples, and in Joshua 24:8, both are said to be Amorites. Genesis 13:7 portrays the Canaanite and the Perizzite as living together in the land. These are just a few references that at first glance may seem confusing and contradictory, but in reality, these peoples may very well be the descendants of Canaan.

Moreover, when the Scriptures refer to the Canaanites, they are referring to either the descendants of Canaan, or the inhabitants of the land, or both, since the inhabitants are not necessarily descendants of Canaan. The Perizzites were first mentioned in Genesis 13:7, but their relation to the Canaanites is not known, other than that they occupied the same land.

God promised Abraham the entire land of Canaan. This land will be divided among his physical seed through Isaac. The twelve tribes of Israel will occupy it during the millennial reign of Christ, and not before, according to Ezekiel, chapters 40 through 48. The Promised Land will include the following countries: Cyprus, Lebanon, present Israel, Egypt and the Sinai Peninsula, Jordan, Syria, the Arabian Peninsula, Iraq, and Kuwait (Genesis 15:18). In the meantime, the Jews might coexist peaceably with their local Arab brethren, but this is wishful and unrealistic thinking (see page 94).

The Jews had done nothing at all to deserve the land of Canaan—they had not acquired it through their love and obedience of God, nor had they won it through their own strength or skill in war. The land was a gift from God. Why? Because that was what he wanted to do in accordance with his prophetic will (Romans 9:17-21).

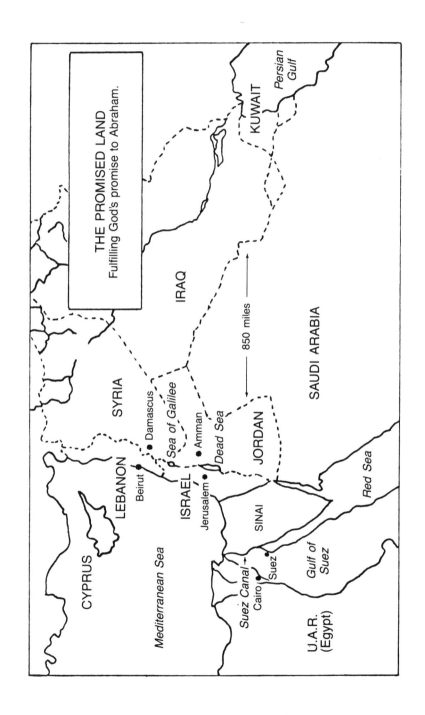

THE PROMISED LAND
Fulfilling God's promise to Abraham.

CYPRUS

Mediterranean Sea

LEBANON

Beirut

SYRIA

Damascus

Sea of Galilee

ISRAEL

Jerusalem

Amman

Dead Sea

JORDAN

IRAQ

KUWAIT

Persian Gulf

850 miles

SAUDI ARABIA

SINAI

Suez Canal

Cairo

Suez

Gulf of Suez

Red Sea

U.A.R. (Egypt)

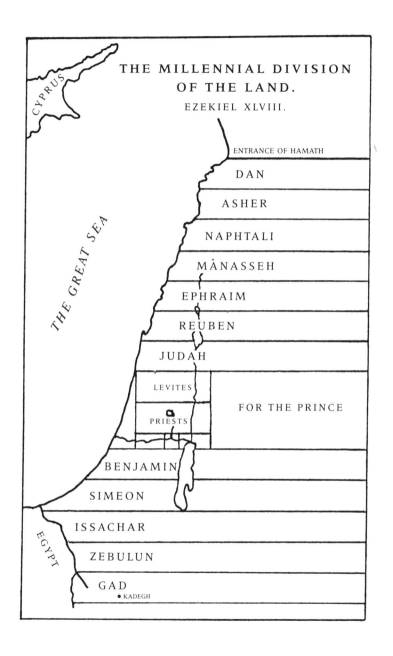

THE MILLENNIAL DIVISION
OF THE LAND.

EZEKIEL XLVIII.

CYPRUS

ENTRANCE OF HAMATH

DAN

ASHER

NAPHTALI

MANASSEH

EPHRAIM

REUBEN

JUDAH

THE GREAT SEA

LEVITES

PRIESTS

FOR THE PRINCE

BENJAMIN

SIMEON

ISSACHAR

EGYPT

ZEBULUN

GAD

• KADEGH

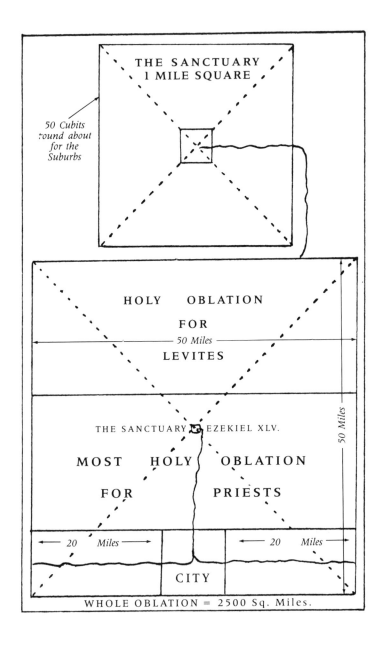

THE SANCTUARY
1 MILE SQUARE

50 Cubits
round about
for the
Suburbs

HOLY   OBLATION

FOR

← 50 Miles →

LEVITES

50 Miles

THE SANCTUARY ▭ EZEKIEL XLV.

MOST   HOLY   OBLATION

FOR   PRIESTS

← 20   Miles →   ← 20   Miles →

CITY

WHOLE OBLATION = 2500 Sq. Miles.

Noah's thrilling prophecy concerning the land of Canaan has been regretfully overlooked by most Bible scholars. In fact, the Scripture passage, Genesis 9:20-27, has been and still is plaguing Bible students, mainly because it is so difficult to understand why Canaan received the blame for his father's sin. Since the Bible does not teach that curses fall indiscriminately upon the heads of the innocent, different explanations have been offered for the reason Canaan was cursed, and not Ham. Some have suggested that the curse is applicable to the black race because of the historical evidence of their servitude and present ethnic predicament. Others maintain that Noah cursed Canaan because Ham's moral guilt would manifest itself in Canaan and his posterity. A third view, which I propose, concerns the land of Canaan and is not necessarily related to him personally or to his descendants.

It is imperative to point out at this time that the whole passage of Genesis 9:20-27 cannot possibly be considered here in a critical fashion, for that would be a dissertation in itself. However, there is one critical point that it is important to discuss, and that is whether the prophetic utterance of Noah's curse relates to Canaan and his descendants, or to the Promised Land. More often than not, a reader loses the main thought of the account if the setting of the curse passage is not explained in narrative form; following is a very brief and simple version of the passage:

Noah emerged from the ark and returned to his former employment as a farmer. He planted a vineyard, and when the harvest had come, he drank his fermented wine, became drunk, and uncovered his nakedness within his tent. When Ham saw his father in that deplorable state, he probably made light of what he saw and told his brothers about it. His brothers went into the tent, walking backward, and, without looking at their father's shame, respectfully covered him. When Noah returned to consciousness, he knew either by inquiry or by special revelation, what his younger son had done. Then, instead of cursing Ham, the guilty party, Noah uttered a most profound biblical prophecy in relation to the land of Canaan.

God has already cursed the earth for Adam's sin of disobedience (Genesis 3:17-19), but Noah's curse on Canaan has a far-reaching implication concerning the Promised Land.

Grammatical Consideration of the Curse

In Genesis 9:25, Noah said, "cursed be Canaan." The verbal noun here is a passive participle from the root *to curse*. The participle in the active voice emphasizes continuous action. The passive voice suggests action happening to the subject. The continuous action is taking place on Canaan, the subject of the verbal noun clause. The participle stresses a durative quality, pointing not only to Canaan, but also pointing, by implication, to his land as well.

I believe that God was preparing the scene for chapter 12, when he called Abraham and promised the land of Canaan to his physical seed, the twelve tribes of Israel.

The Holy Land

The Bible says that "all the earth" is God's, "and they that dwell therein" (Exodus 19:5; Psalm 24:1). However, there is something special about the land of Canaan. God chose it for a very specific reason. The land belongs to God, and he chose the Jews to fulfill his prophetic plan, beginning with the Exodus and ending with the millennial reign of Christ. God brought the Jews to "his land," but they defiled it (Jeremiah 2:7), mainly because they, like all of us, are totally depraved.

On my recent missionary journey to Israel, I met several evangelical Christians who had come from America to tour the "holy land." However, I was astonished to learn that none of those I talked to had come to evangelize the Arabs or the Jews. They were excited to have the opportunity to tour the land and visit the biblical places set apart for worshiping God. I was surprised when I was told they had to pay unfair prices to enter those places. I am reminded of what the Lord Jesus said on a similar occasion: "My house shall be called of all nations the house of prayer, but ye have made it a den of thieves" (Mark 11:17; cf. Isaiah 56:7).

Furthermore, Canaan has been erroneously called the Holy

Land. There is nothing holy about the land itself. In fact, many unholy things have been practiced on it, and the blood of martyrs that was shed and shall be shed there will continue to cry out from the ground (Luke 11:47-51; cf. Revelation 6:10, 14:18-20). The Bible identifies it as the Promised Land, not the Holy Land (Genesis 15:18). Although God cursed the ground in Genesis 3:17, the Promised Land shall become holy when our Holy Lord Jesus sets up his Kingdom in Jerusalem during the forthcoming millennial reign. Then "all nations shall serve him" (Psalm 72:8, 11).

This was the land that saw the heart of God revealed through his Son Jesus Christ, and through his prophets and servants. It was there that many heard the matchless teachings of Jesus and witnessed his miracles. It was there that he was rejected and crucified by "all the house of Israel" (Acts 2:36). It was there that he was buried for three days, was resurrected bodily from the grave, and was seen by several hundreds of his followers before he ascended to heaven (I Corinthians 15:3-8).

This is also the land where the final world events will take place and the last great battles will be fought (Revelation 16:13-16). God has already brought his prophetic clock, the Jews, back to Israel to prepare the last scene for the final act which will bring the world into the "great tribulation" (Matthew 24:21). Thereafter, the Lord Jesus will return to "his land" to reign on this earth for "one thousand years" (Revelation 20:6)!

The Great Tribulation

The first purpose of the great tribulation is to purge the nation Israel for rejecting and crucifying the Messiah. Although Christ voluntarily went to the cross to pay the full penalty "for the sins of the world" (I John 2:2), God holds the Jewish nation accountable for crucifying his Son, and for requesting that "his blood be on us, and on our children" (Matthew 27:25). He came to the Jews first, but "his own received him not" (John 1:11). And when Pilate asked, "What shall I do then with Jesus which is called Christ? They all say unto him, Let him be crucified" (Matthew 27:22). In Peter's anointed sermon at Pentecost, he proclaimed that the Jews were guilty of crucifying the Lord: "Therefore, let all the house of Israel know assuredly, that God hath made that same Jesus, whom ye have crucified, both Lord and Christ" (Acts 2:36, 4:10). Stephen also, in his powerful narrative, charged the Jews with killing the prophets of God and crucifying the Savior. He reminded them that they had provoked God to wrath in the Old Testament, that they had rejected and crucified their Messiah, and they even stoned him to death for telling them the truth:

> Ye stiffnecked and uncircumcised in heart and ears, ye do always resist the Holy Ghost: as your fathers did, so do ye. Which of the prophets have not your fathers persecuted? and they have slain them which shewed before of the coming of the Just One; of whom ye have been now the betrayers and murderers. . . . When they heard these things . . . they gnashed on him with their teeth. . . . And cast him out of the city, and stoned him (Acts 7:51-58).

Moreover, God's judgment on Israel shall be much more severe than on all other nations—for many additional reasons: "chiefly, because that unto them were committed the oracles of God" (Romans 3:2), and also because much more knowledge of God was bestowed on them, and of them "shall be much required" (Luke 12:48). However, when the Jews rejected the Messiah, God gave them "the spirit of slumber", and "through their fall salvation is come unto the Gentiles, for to provoke them to jealousy" (Romans 11:8, 11). Meanwhile, all who "have received the Spirit of adoption" (Romans 8:15) through faith in Christ Jesus are now called the chosen people of God. We are "chosen of God, and precious . . . an holy priesthood, to offer up spiritual sacrifices, acceptable to God by Jesus Christ. . . . Which in time past were not a people, but are now the people of God" (I Peter 2:4-5, 10)!

Conversely, in the great tribulation God intends to purge the nation of Israel, preparing a "remnant" of Jews to receive the Messiah "whom they have pierced" (Zechariah 12:10). The Bible teaches that only some will receive salvation during the tribulation. God said, "I will bring the third part through the fire, and will refine them as silver is refined, and will try them as gold is tried" (Zechariah 13:9). To affirm this truth, Paul quoted Isaiah 10:22: "Though the number of the children of Israel be as the sand of the sea, a remnant shall be saved" (Romans 9:27). As John the Baptist preached in the spirit of Elijah to prepare Israel for the first coming of the Messiah (Matthew 11:14; Mark 1:3), God will use the 144,000 Jews during the great tribulation to prepare the way for his second coming (Revelation 7:4). These same evangelists will be martyred for their uncompromising faith in Christ, and through their bold evangelism, many Jews and Gentiles shall be saved (Revelation 7:9, 14); the "gospel of the kingdom shall be preached in all the world . . . and then shall the end come" (Matthew 24:14; cf. Revelation 14:1-4).

The second purpose of the great tribulation is "to punish the inhabitants of the earth for their iniquity" (Isaiah 26:21; Revelation 3:10). God holds man accountable for rejecting the free gift of salvation by faith in Christ Jesus. He will pour out his wrath upon all unbelieving Jews and Gentiles, because "God is no respecter of persons" (Jeremiah 25:29-33; Matthew 24:21, 25:31-46; Acts 10:34; I Thessalonians 2:12; Revelation 6:12-17). In describing the great tribulation (Revelation 9:20), the following terms are never used in the positive: Father, grace, hope, faith, love, peace, pray, and comfort. The absence of these terms indicates that the great tribulation will be a time of sadness and unparalleled suffering.

The Fig Tree

The fig tree symbolizes Israel. Chapter 24 of Jeremiah contains a vivid picture of the scattering and regathering of the Jews, clearly seen in verses 5 through 10. The bad figs refer to the dispersing of Israel, and the good figs refer to the regathering of the remnant of Jews. Because the Lord Jesus had been rejected as Messiah, he cursed the fruit of the fig tree, and the visible part of the tree dried up (Mark 11:14, 20). The root, or the seed, of the fig tree was not cursed, but only the fruit. God chose the Jews to be his "witnesses," but they disobeyed him and rejected his salvation (Isaiah 43:10). Therefore, the Lord Jesus predicted that the fruit of the fig tree was placed under a temporary curse, and that prior to his second return to earth, the fig tree will begin to bud once more. Although the Jews were dispersed among all the nations for their rebellion and unbelief (Deuteronomy 28:63-68), the Lord Jesus promised to regather a remnant of them in his land to prepare them for the great tribulation (Ezekiel 36:18-27; Zechariah 12:3). And the generation that will witness the budding of the fig tree (the return of the Jews to the Promised Land) may also suffer during the great tribulation, before the consummation of the end-times, as prophesied in Matthew 24, Mark 13, and Luke 21. It is amazing that the "fig tree" has survived all these centuries without producing fruit. This miraculous preservation of Israel is another proof that nothing can alter or hinder God's sovereign prophetic plan.

According to my understanding of God's plan for Israel, I have listed the seven stages of growth of the fig tree:

1. The curse on the fruit of the fig tree has been lifted, according to Matthew 24:32. The branches of the fig tree began to put forth leaves when Israel became a nation on May 14, 1948. I believe that Ezekiel 37:10-12 was also fulfilled when God put meat on the dry bones, symbolizing the rebirth of the physical Israel. The tender branch and the putting forth of leaves refer to the return of a remnant of Jews to the Promised Land.

2. When a male child is born, he must be circumcized on the eighth day (Genesis 17:12). Circumcision is a badge, or mark, of separation unto God. In Luke 2:21 we see the Lord Jesus fulfilling his prophetic role by being circumcized on the eighth day. The nation of Israel was born on May 14, 1948, but the War of Independence was fought for eight bloody days, and on the twenty-second of the same month, the newly born nation became separated prophetically unto God.

3. In the next phase the young boy becomes accountable to God at the age of twelve. The Lord Jesus fulfilled prophecy at the age of twelve by teaching in the Jerusalem temple (Luke 2:42). The United Nations recognized the accountability of Israel as a result of the Eichmann Affair. When Israel was about twelve years old in 1961, God delivered Adolf Eichmann into the hands of the Jews. Eichmann was accused of being instrumental in burning to death more than six million Jews in Germany during World War II. He was tried and executed in Israel in 1962.

4. The accountable young lad becomes a strong man of war at the age of twenty. God commanded Moses to prepare armies of men twenty years old, "all that are able to go forth to war in Israel" (Numbers 1:3, 26:2). The recovery of Jerusalem during the Six Day War in June of 1967 may very well be the prophetic fulfillment of the fig tree becoming fruitful again. When we study prophecy, we must use the Jewish calendar. The year is comprised of twelve months, and each month has thirty days. When we add twenty years to May 14, 1948, we arrive at the approximate date of the Six Day War of June 1967. As I said previously, God has already brought back a remnant of unbelieving Jews to prepare the way for the great tribulation. Jerusalem was created "in the midst of the nations" (Ezekiel 5:5), and since the time of Abraham, many nations have tried in vain to retain possession of it. Jerusalem is the Lord's capital city. He "will gather all nations against Jerusalem to do battle" during the great tribulation (Zechariah 14:2), and then the Lord Jesus will return to earth to rule the world from Jerusalem for one thousand years (Zechariah 14:3-11; Revelation 20:4).

5. According to God's prophetic will, his chosen servants are not allowed to serve him until they reach the age of thirty (Numbers 4:3). Joseph started his ministry in Egypt at the age of thirty (Genesis 41:46). David became king of Israel and began his reigh when he was "thirty years old" (II Samuel 5:4). The Lord Jesus launched his ministry when he was "about thirty years of age" (Luke 3:23). Israel signed a peace treaty with Egypt at the same age, thirty, to prepare the way for

the Antichrist, who will ratify this same treaty when God chooses to reveal him (Daniel 9:27).

6. "This generation shall not pass, till all these things be fulfilled" (Matthew 24:34). According to the Old Testament, a generation is usually forty, fifty, or one hundred years. However, the Lord Jesus is not speaking here about years, but about the nation of Israel. The Greek word for generation is *genus*, meaning *family* or *race*. In other words, the Lord is saying that the Jewish race will continue to be his prophetic time clock until the end of the millennial reign.

7. "Heaven and earth shall pass away, but my words shall not pass away" (Matthew 24:35). God fulfills his plans according to "the immutability of his counsel" (Hebrews 6:17; Revelation 17:17). The Bible teaches that the Lord Jesus will return with his saints to set up his millennial kingdom in Jerusalem. During that time, the twelve Apostles will rule over the twelve tribes of Israel, and King David will rule over them all in the land of Canaan, under the divine supervision of the Lord and Savior Jesus Christ (Matthew 19:27, 28; Luke 22:30; cf. Isaiah 2:1-6, 11:6-12; Ezekiel 34:23-30, 37:24-28; Revelation 3:21, 5:10, 21:12-14). The millennium will be a time of unusual spiritual blessing, because God shall pour out his Holy Spirit "upon all flesh" (Joel 2:28-29), and the whole "earth shall be full of the knowledge of the Lord" (Isaiah 11:9). All earthly people who have survived the great tribulation and been redeemed by the blood of the Lamb will enter the blessedness of the millennium (Revelaion 20:4). However, the descendants of the redeemed will be born with a sinful nature, and salvation by faith in Christ will be required of them. That is the main reason God will retain Satan—so that he can use him once more at the end of the thousand years.

After the millennium, God shall judge all unbelieving Jews and Gentiles (Revelation 20:7-15) and shall destroy "the first heaven and the first earth" (II Peter 3:10; Revelation 21:1). The "new Jerusalem," the eternal community of saints, or the Bride of Christ, shall inhabit "a new heaven and a new earth," and God "will dwell with them and they shall be his people"

(Revelation 21:1-3). Only then will the fig tree cease to represent Israel as God's prophetic clock; it shall be replaced by the eternal prophetic "tree of life," symbol of everlasting peace and joy for all who have been redeemed by the blood of Jesus Christ, shed on the cross at Calvary (Revelation 22:2, 14, 19).

Armageddon

Armageddon derives from the Hebrew *har Megiddo*, meaning *hill* or *city* of Megiddo, also called the valley of Jezreel, or Esdraelon. This valley stretches between the mountains of Galilee in the north and the mountains of Samaria in the south, in the shape of a triangle (15 by 15 by 20 miles). It is the most famous battlefield in the world. More than twenty wars have been fought there, including Barak's victory over the Canaanites (Judges 4:15) and Gideon's over the Midianites (Judges 7). It was also there that Saul and Josiah died (I Samuel 31:8; II Chronicles 35:22). The last war was fought in that valley when General Allenby defeated the Ottoman Turks and captured Jerusalem on December 11, 1917, without firing a shot. However, the final and bloodiest battle, Armageddon, shall be fought by the Lord Jesus at his advent of glory, against the Antichrist and the Gentile world powers (Revelation 16:16). During that time, God shall bring all these world powers to that valley in order to crush them with the fire of his wrath; and blood will be splattered over the land of Israel for a distance of two hundred miles (Revelation 14:18-20)—the length of the entire state of Israel. All unbelieving Jews and Gentiles shall suffer greatly in those days. The Lord Jesus said, "For there shall be great tribulation, such as was not since the beginning of the world to this time, no, nor ever shall be" (Matthew 24:21). In fact, "in those days shall men seek death, and shall not find it; and shall desire to die, and death shall flee from them" (Revelation 9:6).

The Bible predicts that two horrible future world wars will occur before the Lord's second return to earth. Both wars will be fought in Israel, because God has already determined to "gather all nations against Jerusalem to battle" (Zephaniah

3:8; Zechariah 14:2). First he will cause the powerful army of the North Eastern Confederacy to invade the land; then he will annihilate them. The Bible gives the following reason for God's righteous action: "And thou shalt come up against my people of Israel, as a cloud to cover the land; it shall be in the latter days, and I will bring thee against my land, that the heathen may know me. . . . And I will be known in the eyes of many nations, and they shall know that I am the Lord" (Ezekiel 38:16, 23).

Second, God will gather the forces of the Antichrist and the armies of East Asia "into a place called in the Hebrew tongue Armageddon" (Revelation 16:16), and he will destroy them also. It is so exciting to be on God's side and not have to worry about the consequences of his wrath. No one has ever been able to fathom God's prophetic sovereign will. God always does what he pleases, and he has given us the free will and the privilege to obey him. The following verses explain the reason for the great tribulation, ending with the final world war before the millennial reign of Christ:

> For, lo, I begin to bring evil on the city which is called by my name, and should ye be utterly unpunished? Ye shall not be unpunished: for I will call for a sword upon all the inhabitants of the earth, saith the *Lord* of hosts. Therefore prophesy thou against them all these words, and say unto them, The *Lord* shall roar from on high, and utter his voice from his holy habitation; he shall mightily roar upon his habitation; he shall give a shout, as they that tread *the grapes*, against all the inhabitants of the earth. A noise shall come *even* to the ends of the earth; for the *Lord* hath a controversy with the nations, he will plead with all flesh; he will give them *that are* wicked to the sword, saith the *Lord*. Thus saith the *Lord* of hosts, Behold, evil shall go forth from nation to nation, and a great whirlwind shall be raised up from the coasts of the earth. And the slain of the *Lord* shall be at that day from *one*

end of the earth even unto the *other* end of the
earth: they shall not be lamented, neither gathered,
nor buried; they shall be dung upon the ground
(Jeremiah 25:29-33).

These verses clearly teach that God is angry with all
unbelieving Jews and Gentiles. The only way to escape God's
wrath is to believe on his Son. John the Baptist said, "He that
believeth on the Son hath everlasting life: and he that believeth
not the Son shall not see life; but the wrath of God abideth on
him" (John 3:36).

King of the North

According to my understanding of God's future prophetic
plan for mankind, the entire world will be divided into three
international alignments of nations. These three Gentile con-
federacies will gather around them a number of allies, and
their burning desire will be to contest supremacy for world
control. The ultimate goal of all ungodly world powers has
been to totally dominate the earth. History teaches that only a
few nations were able to control the world for a specific
prophetic reason. For instance, Persia, Greece, Rome, the Arab
Caliphs, and England were able to control the world. Those
five empires had one major thing in common—each ruled
Egypt and dominated the Mediterranean Sea.

Many powers came close to controlling the earth, but failed
because they were unable to take Egypt. Two great world wars
ended in defeat for Germany, after that nation had gained
phenomenal land and air victories, mainly because the British
retained control of Egypt and the Allies retained control of
the Mediterranean. There is something special about Egypt.
Through all recorded history, Egypt has been considered the
most important strategic location on earth. In addition to its
historical civilization and great wealth, Egypt is the gateway
to three continents: Asia, Europe, and Africa. Prophetically
speaking, Egypt represents the Arab countries and their
wealth. The Middle East possesses more than half the total

proven oil reserves of the world, or about three times that of the United States. Access to Arab oil is vital to the world's survival. Possession of Egypt by a predominant sea power makes it possible for that power to control the world.

These facts have long been understood by the masters of the Kremlin. They know how strategic the Middle East is to any would-be world conqueror. For several decades Russia has been exerting much energy toward that end. Their utter belief in atheism, so abhorrent to Islam's monotheism has kept them from succeeding. However, when God helped Israel win the Six Day War, Russia was able to materialize her long-awaited dream.

One British reporter wrote, "Israel had bloodied the nose of the Russians." It was a logical deduction for western mentality that because the Arabs had lost the war in June of 1967, Russia was defeated also. On the contrary, Russia was very pleased to see the Arabs lose in the most embarrassing and humiliating way possible, in order to convince the vast Muslim world that America and her Allies were irrevocably pledged to the political support of Israel. The Russian leaders proved their point to the Arabs, and after some diplomatic maneuvering, Egypt, Syria, and Iraq signed a secret pact with Russia.

I find it most exciting to be living in a day when so many prophecies are being fulfilled with a breathtaking accuracy before my eyes. God says that he will put hooks into Russia's jaws and will bring her to the Mideast to take a spoil (oil, mineral wealth of the Dead Sea, the Suez Canal, and much more). In fact, the entire world is moving methodically toward the inevitable two holocaustal wars. However, there is in the western world a strange sense of invincibility and false security, and a widespread belief that things are bound to improve. But the Bible says the opposite, and the signs are all around us to substantiate these prophetic truths (I Thessalonians 5:1-3; II Thessalonians 1:6-10).

Chapters 38 and 39 of Ezekiel give a detailed description of the first future world war. God's prophet identifies the nations that must participate in the inescapable conflict and points out the exact location of the invasion. It is interesting to note that these predictions were proclaimed more than twenty-five hundred years ago. The infallible and inerrant Word of God instructed Ezekiel to predict Russia's invasion of Israel long before Russia became a nation, and after Israel went into Babylonian captivity.

The most significant result of this chain of events is that after the physical restoration of Israel, and before the spiritual rebirth of the remnant Jews, the North Eastern Confederacy will invade Israel. Israel has already been physically restored; and since 1948, the land has been rebuilt "without walls, and having neither bars nor gates" (Ezekiel 38:11). God is preparing Israel to be invaded, and he will use her as bait to attract the exploiters "to take a spoil, and to take a prey" (Ezekiel 38:12). God is planning to bring the armies of his choice to Israel, to destroy them after they reach the zenith of their strength. Because unbelievers have rejected the only Lord and Savior, Jesus Christ, God "will make Jerusalem a cup of trembling unto all the people. . . . And in that day . . . all that burden themselves with it shall be cut in pieces, though all the people of the earth be gathered together against it" (Zechariah 12:2, 3).

Gog and Magog

Hebrew lexicons identify Magog as the country of Russia. Magog, Tubal, and Mesheck, mentioned in Ezekiel 38:2, were the second, fifth, and sixth sons of Japheth (Genesis 10:2). The renowned Jewish historians Flavius Josephus (34–95 A.D.) and Wilhelm Gesenius (1786–1842) both agree that Magog was the founder of the Magogites, whom the Greeks called Scythians. These Japhethites left Mt. Ararat, where Noah's ark rested after the flood, and have been traced by those reliable historians to modern Russia.

Gog refers to the end-time ruler or leader, and Magog is the land over which Gog will rule. He will lead his nation and his Allies to Israel, where he shall be buried with "all his multitude" (Ezekiel 39:11). On the basis of Daniel 11:40, this leader is referred to as "the king of the north," because he will soon make a surprise move against Israel from his homeland "out of the north parts" (Ezekiel 38:15). The Hebrew word Rosh, which occurs in verses 2 and 3 in Ezekiel, chapter 38, refers to modern Russia. Russia was known to the Greeks as Rucia. The word Rosh is also found in the *Codex Sinaiticus,* one of the most ancient copies of the original manuscripts.

Meshech became known as Mosoch, then Muscovy, and during the time of Ivan the Terrible (1533–1584), who ruled as Czar of Russia, the name was changed to Moscow. Tubal became known as modern Tubolks, a city in southwestern Siberia. It is interesting to note that Magog is said to be China, or Mongolia, in the Aramaic Bible, but Gog and Magog have been clearly identified by the Word of God as the modern country of Russia.

Ezekiel identifies the nations that will come with Russia to invade Israel: "Persia, Ethiopia, and Libya . . . Gomer . . . the house of Togarmah of the north quarters" (Ezekiel 38:5-6).

Persia

Although Persia changed its name to Iran in 1932, I believe the Lord is speaking here of the Persian Empire circa 500 B.C., which extended from the Indus River on the east to the Tigris on the west. This army may include the nations of Iran, Kurdistan, Afghanistan, Pakistan, some of the Arabs states of the Persian Gulf and the Arabian Peninsula, Greece, Cyprus, Lebanon, Syria, and Egypt, and their offspring.

God used the Iranian crisis in 1980, when some fifty-two Americans were held hostage for 444 days, to allow Russia to invade Afghanistan and to indoctrinate Iran for the invasion of Israel. I remember vividly when the American government tried in vain to rescue the hostages by sending highly trained soldiers to wait in Egypt. They were then flown to a designated desert location in Iran, not far from Tehran. Finally, when the order came for them to take off, more than one helicopter caught fire, killing and injuring several soldiers, and destroying all human hope for the rescue.

Ironically, the media blamed the government for the failure. The government blamed the engines of the aircrafts. And the rescuers blamed the weather. The truth of the matter is that God resists anyone who interferes with his prophetic plan. The rescue team should not be blamed for the mission's failure. Neither should the powerful engines or the almost perfect weather be blamed. The main reason for the unsuccessful rescue mission should be attributed to God. Just a few seconds before the helicopters were to take off, God sent a strong sand storm to stop the rescue operation.

The inscrutable recent turmoil in Lebanon has also confused the wisdom of the world. However, I believe Lebanon symbolizes idolatry and self-sufficiency. The Lord is using Lebanon as an example to warn all ungodly nations of their pending disaster. God said, "And I will prepare destroyers against thee, every one with his weapons: and they shall cut down thy choice cedars, and cast them into the fire" (Jeremiah 22:7). The Bible also predicts that the violence done to Lebanon will also be done to the heathens. "For the violence of Lebanon shall cover thee" (Habakkuk 2:17).

Egypt will get the same treatment, and God "will set the Egyptians against the Egyptians: and they shall fight every one against his brother, and every one against his neighbor; city against city, and kingdom against kingdom" (Isaiah 19:2). Nevertheless, because it was in Egypt that Joseph prospered; because it was in Egypt that the children of Israel were welcomed; and because it was in Egypt that the Lord Jesus found shelter until the death of King Herod, God will bless Egypt during the millennium, "saying, Blessed be Egypt my people" (Isaiah 19:25). Perhaps Egypt represents the remnant Arabs who will believe in the Messiah.

Ethiopia

The Hebrew word for Ethiopia is Kush. Cush was the eldest son of Ham and the progenitor of the black race (Genesis 10:6). He has been identified with the continent of Africa, and all of Africa was known to the Greeks as Ethiopia. The Cushites mixed with other races, as has been mentioned, and may have been Semitized through intermarriage. Jeremiah 13:23 seems to support this view: "Can the Ethiopian change his skin?"

According to *Young's Analytical Concordance to the Bible,* the name Ethiopia is used in Scripture nine times to refer to the area in southern Africa, and eleven times to refer to the land of Cush, an area in northern Africa.

Libya

Libya has been identified with Phut, the third son of Ham (Genesis 10:6). It may include present day Libya, Morocco, Tunisia, Algeria, and their Berber offspring.

Gomer

The Jewish Talmud, a collection of law and tradition, states that Gomer settled in Germany. He was the eldest son of Japheth (Genesis 10:2) and may represent all European communist nations.

Togarmah

Armenian literature refers to the land and its people as "the House of Togarmah." God said that Togarmah, a son of Gomer (Genesis 10:3), will come with Russia from "the north quarters, and all his bands: and many people" (Ezekiel 38:6). Togarmah may include the Turkoman tribes of central Asia, the Tartars, the Mongols, the Turks, and the Armenians.

This powerful army with its highly sophisticated weapons will soon fall upon "the land that is brought back from the sword, and is gathered out of many people, against the mountains of Israel, which have been always waste: but it is brought forth out of the nations, and they shall dwell safely . . . all of them dwelling without walls, and having neither bars nor gates, to take a spoil, and to take a prey." (Ezekiel 38:8-12).

This refers to the first future world war, which shall be fought in Israel prior to the Lord's return to earth. Ezekiel is describing the rebirth of physical Israel and the rebuilding of the nation. Since 1948, the cities have been rebuilt without the traditional towering walls, thick bar lines, and sturdy gates. These were used for protection, but modern Israel is now ripe for future enemy invasions.

Western Alliance

After God destroys Russia and her followers with a master stroke "upon the mountains of Israel" (Ezekiel 39:4), he will energize and mobilize "Sheba, and Dedan, and the merchants of Tarshish, with the young lions thereof" (Ezekiel 38:13).

I believe that Sheba and Dedan represent the Druze sect presently living in Israel. It is interesting to note that many religious Druze leaders take much pride in their ability to trace their origin to ancient Yemen. The Yemen has already been identified with Sheba, one of the thirteen Arab tribes which descended from Joktan (Genesis 10:28). Some leaders also believe that they are the seed of Abraham through Keturah's second son, Jokshan. Sheba and Dedan are the sons of Jokshan (Genesis 25:3). Moreover, thousands of Druze had settled in Palestine long before the physical rebirth of Israel in 1948. Now they number more than sixty thousand who have chosen to align themselves with Israel permanently and to fight side by side with the Jews. Since the Druze community has been conditioned to believe that they may be one of the lost tribes of Israel, and since they are accepted neither by the Christian Arabs nor by the Muslims, they have decided to become loyal to their host country, Israel. Most make their homes in the mountainous regions of Israel's Upper Galilee and Mt. Carmel. They have also been given many other privileges, and they speak with excessive pride of possessing equality with the Jews. Therefore I believe that the Israeli Druze will be the only Arabs at peace with the Jews in the forthcoming world wars. In fact, everyone else will turn against Israel during the great tribulation. The Lord Jesus warned the believing Jewish remnant that they "shall be hated of all nations" (Matthew 10:22, 24:9).

Merchants of Tarshish

"Merchants of Tarshish" is a biblical term employed in connection with warships and commercial ships. Tarshish is a Phoenician word meaning *sea merchants* and *traders*. The Canaanites in Lebanon were named Phoenicians by the Greeks because of the purple-dyed textiles they traded. The purple dye was derived from shellfish in the waters of Lebanon's seashore, the throat of each shellfish producing only one drop of the dye. The purple-garment industry was very costly due to the painstaking procedure of extracting the dye from the shellfish. The Phoenicians trimmed their textile products with it and wove it into their rugs and tapestries.

The Phoenicians gave the western world its alphabet and were the first shipbuilders to cross the Mediterranean and the Atlantic in search of gold, tin, copper, and iron ore (Ezekiel 27:12). They helped Solomon build his ships and train his navy in "knowledge of the sea" (I Kings 9:27, 10:22). Moreover, Jonah probably fled from God on one of these ships (Jonah 1:3); and Jehoshaphat tried in vain to build ships like those of Solomon, to fetch gold from India (I Kings 22:48).

Around 1000 b.c. the Phoenicians founded Gades (modern Gibraltar), a town on the southern rocky tip of Spain. However, of all their colonies, Carthage (modern Tunisia) was the most important, mainly because it became the center of world trade during that time. It was the gateway between the Middle East, Europe, and Africa. The Phoenicians sailed to England in search of tin, and they may have discovered many lands long before the dates claimed by Europeans. Both Christopher Columbus and Amerigo Vespucci used maritime skills and geographic knowledge developed by the genius of the Phoenicians. Those two explorers were commissioned by Queen Isabella and King Ferdinand of Spain. Spain was credited with the discovery of the Americas, but the Phoenicians contributed the basic crafts required for such great accomplishments. They were not only the best shipbuilders and navigators, but also have been credited with many land discoveries. In addition to Gades and Carthage, they colonized the island of Sardinia (near Italy), Tartassos (modern Cadiz), and others. Some reliable Bible scholars and historians link Tarshish with Tartassos, a city in southern Spain which the Phoenicians used as a seaport for cargo ships. Tarshish was the second son of Javan and a grandson of Japheth (Genesis 10:4). He probably founded Spain, and Spain became identified with sea merchants and traders. In the absence of air and ground transportation, commercial ships were the only means of efficient world trade and prosperity. Tartassos became known as Cadiz, and Cadiz became a mecca for the merchants of Tarshish. Hence, Tarshish is called Tartassos in Spain and was referred to by ancient poets to express the extreme west.

Long after the Phoenicians disappeared from the scene, England and Spain became world powers and dominated the waters with their naval fleets and commercial ships. In this sense, they may be considered the leaders of "the merchants of Tarshish" and the progenitors of "all the young lions" (Ezekiel 38:13). In other words, the merchants of Tarshish could very well be identified with the western powers of the modern Common Market, whose livelihood is utterly dependent upon commercial world trade and a promising economic system. On the other hand, the young lions may represent the descendants of the Common Market nations who have emigrated and colonized foreign lands—the Americas, Australia, New Zealand, and all their isles (coastlands).

This Western Alliance will be forced to unite under one unique system of government, controlled and manipulated by a most powerful and ingenious leader, "that man of sin" (II Thessalonians 2:3). He will mesmerize his followers with satanic "power and signs and lying wonders" (II Thessalonians 2:9). God will allow this Antichrist to deceive those people who do not have in their hearts a genuine desire for "the truth, that they might be saved" (II Thessalonians 2:10). Unregenerate persons have always been deceived by counterfeit supernatural miracles. During the forthcoming great tribulation, the manifestations of Satan's power will be much greater than ever before. As a result of man's stubborn rejection of the gospel of Christ, which "is the power of God unto salvation to every one that believeth" (Romans 1:16), God also will reject them. "And for this cause God shall send them strong delusion that they should believe a lie: That they all might be damned who believe not the truth, but had pleasure in unrighteousness" (II Thessalonians 2:11-12).

The Bible teaches that all unbelieving Jews and Gentiles living under the leadership of the Antichrist will worship him (Revelation 13:8). They will also "receive a mark in their right hand, or in their foreheads: And that no man might buy or sell, save he that had the mark, or the name of the beast, or the number of his name. . . . And his number is Six hundred threescore and six" (Revelation 13:16-18). In other words, all the people who pledge allegiance to the Antichrist will be identified by being stamped with the number 666. However,

if any man worship the beast and his image, and receive his mark in his forehead, or in his hand, the same shall drink of the wine of the wrath of God, which is poured out without mixture into the cup of his indignation; and he shall be tormented with fire and brimstone in the presence of the holy angels, and in the presence of the Lamb: And the smoke of their torment ascendeth up for ever and ever: and they have no rest day nor night, who worship the beast and his image, and whosoever receiveth the mark of his name (Revelation 14:9-11).

The Antichrist will keep track of his followers through their identification numbers, while the Lord God "calleth his own sheep by name" (John 10:3). The Antichrist will come "to steal, and to kill, and to destroy," but the Christ came to give us life, that we "might have it more abundantly" (John 10:10). The Antichrist will lead his followers to the eternal "lake of fire" (Revelation 20:15), while the followers of Jesus Christ "shall inherit all things" (Revelation 21:7).

Kings of the East

The word *east* differs in meaning and application in both Hebrew and Greek. The Hebrew word *kedem* means that which is *immediately before* or *in front of* something or someone. Kuddam is the Arabic word for *kedem* and has the same meaning. Kedem is used in a geographic connotation, to describe a location or country immediately before another in an easterly direction. For instance, after Abraham gave many gifts to his Arabian sons through his second wife, Keturah, he sent them on their way "eastward, unto the east country" (Genesis 25:6). Abraham was in Canaan (Palestine) at that time, and he directed his sons and their families toward the land lying immediately to the east of Palestine—Arabia and Mesopotamia (modern Iraq).

On the other hand, *mizrach* is another Hebrew word denoting *east,* meaning the place from which the sun rises. Therefore we see that this word has the connotation of the Far East. For example, Isaiah, using the word *mizrach,* predicted that Cyrus would come down to Jerusalem from the east to liberate the Jews from their bondage in Babylon (Isaiah 41:25, 44:28). Cyrus, who will be a type of Christ, shall return to rescue the believing remnant of Jews from the bondage of Satan. Messiah will return "from the way of the east. . . . And the glory of the *Lord* came into the house by the way of the gate whose prospect is toward the east (Ezekiel 43:2, 4). The Greek word *anatole* and the Latin word *oriens* have the general meaning— *east.* It is assumed that the Near East and Far East are subsumed under the general New Testament Greek word *anatole.*

When we study Bible prophecy, all geographic direction and distance should be determined by locating the points of the compass from Jerusalem. God put Jerusalem "in the midst of the nations and countries that are round about her" (Ezekiel 5:5). Hence the Lord shall harden the hearts of all the nations, "that they should come against Israel in battle, that he might destroy them utterly. . . . And [he] will seek to destroy all the nations that come against Jerusalem" (Joshua 11:20; Zechariah 12:9).

According to the Greek and Hebrew meanings of the word *east,* these oriental kings or rulers may represent all the near and far eastern countries that have not aligned themselves with Russia or with the Antichrist—China, Korea, India, Vietnam, Japan, Jordan, Iraq, Arabia, and others. This multitude of armies shall gather near the eastern banks of the Euphrates river and quickly mobilize their forces in preparation for the final assault on Israel, in order to contest supremacy for world control against the cohorts of the Antichrist.

God "dried up the water of the Red Sea" to deliver Israel from more than four centuries of slavery in Egypt (Joshua 2:10). He dried up the Jordan River to allow "the priests that bare the ark of the covenant of the Lord . . . and all the Israelites" to cross over from Shittim to Jordan (Joshua 3:17). He will also dry up the Euphrates river to allow the armies "of the kings of the east" to cross from Iraq to Israel on dry ground (Revelation 16:12). God is planning to gather all these forces together "into a place called in the Hebrew tongue Armageddon" (Revelation 16:16). The reason for this future final world war is that God has determined to judge all unbelieving Jews and Gentiles prior to his second return to earth. God says to all these nations,

> Assemble yourselves, and come, all ye heathen, and gather yourselves together round about: . . . come up to the valley of Jehoshaphat: for there will I sit to judge all the heathen round about. Put ye in the sickle, for the harvest is ripe: come, get you down; for the press is full, the vats overflow; for their wickedness is great (Joel 3:11-13).

Chapter Four
God's Chosen People

It is generally believed that Arabs, descended from Ishmael, are less important than Jews, mainly because they are the children of Hagar the slave woman, while the Jews are still the chosen race because they descended from Abraham's first wife, Sarah. I have heard this kind of teaching and preaching since 1955, the time of my conversion from Druzism to faith in Christ. In fact, the proponents of this misbelief have flooded the market with a multitude of books on Israel and prophecy, and have succeeded in their feverish drive to condition their political supporters with the idea that Jews are the chosen people of God. Not only that, but for years practically every media of communication in the western world has been propagating this one-sided point of view. As a result, Israel has been pampered and idolized by her allies while the Arabs are being provoked to wrath, and their hearts are hardened against the gospel of Christ. To top it all off, scriptural references relating to Israel have been blown out of proportion and woven into the very fabric of western political theology, in order to justify the superiority of the Jews and to condone the West's political stand with Israel. Consequently, the Arabs' human liberty and security have received little consideration, and their contributions and cultural influence have been intentionally ignored.

The political turmoil in our world today is accentuated by a chronic spiritual disease called racial pride and prejudice. My Lebanese philosophy professor taught me that man will not learn from history. To prove his point, he quoted Hegel, the German philosopher who said, "We ask men to study history, but the only thing that men learn from the study of history is that men learn nothing from the study of history." However, my Lebanese professor and Hegel's Sophistry did not give me the reason man cannot learn from the study of history. Conversely, I believe that racial pride and prejudice are a good reason for this reluctance. Pride and prejudice have inflicted men with much human suffering and will continue to produce hostility and bloodshed between diverse ethnic communities.

This chronic spiritual disease has been inherited from the Adamic sinful nature. It has been acquired and incorporated into all societies through cultural upbringing. Although pride and prejudice could be reduced under certain conditions, they cannot be eradicated. They can be reduced by removing the master-ego and allowing the Lord and Savior Jesus Christ to have total control through the regenerating power of the Holy Spirit. Only then might our inherent attitudes toward our fellowmen be reconditioned.

Nevertheless, the world can no longer afford to keep the truth from being known, or to consciously dismiss biblical and historical facts about the Arabs as guesswork because certain people have been programmed to believe the opposite. It seems to me that the more uncertain people are about the nature and character of God, the more earnestly they search for some passages of Scripture that seem to put him on their side. However, the Bible makes it emphatically clear "that God is no respecter of persons: But in every nation he that feareth him, and worketh righteousness, is accepted with him . . . preaching peace by Jesus Christ . . . that through his name whosoever believeth in him shall receive remission of sins" (Acts 10:34-36, 43).

The Lord Jesus asserted positively that God does not favor one person or race over another; he stressed the fact that God's love is universal and absolutely unbiased: "For God so loved the world, that he gave his only begotten Son, that whosoever believeth in him should not perish, but have everlasting life. . . . He that believeth on me hath everlasting life" (John 3:16, 6:47).

The universality of the gospel is delineated in Matthew's genealogy of the Lord Jesus (Matthew 1:3-6). Tamar, the Canaanite, Rahab, Ruth, and Bathsheba were Gentile women, and they were deliberately mentioned in order to disarm the arrogant pride and prejudice of all orthodox Jews, who were conditioned to believe that they were the chosen people of God.

I believe that it was one of the saddest moments of the Lord's earthly ministry when "he came unto his own, and his own received him not" (John 1:11, 7:5). And throughout his public ministry there was strong opposition and an outright hostility on the part of the Jewish leaders, not only for reaffirming the new covenant of salvation by grace "through faith" (Ephesians 2:8), but also because he claimed to be God in the flesh and the Savior of mankind (John 10:30-33, 14:6). They accused him of having "a devil" (John 7:20) and of being "a sinner" (John 9:24-34). They tried relentlessly to undermine his authority, and on many occasions they "sought to kill him" (John 7:1).

On one of those occasions, he gave them an illustration from the Hebrew Scriptures to demonstrate God's indiscriminate love for the Lebanese and Syrian Arabs, who were considered by the Jews to be inferior and unconverted. During his early public ministry, the Lord Jesus came to Nazareth and entered the synagogue on the Sabbath day. After reading the Messianic prophecy from Isaiah 61:1, "All them that were in the synagogue . . . wondered at the gracious words which proceedeth out of his mouth" (Luke 4:20-22). Subsequently, when he began cutting into the root of their problem of pride and prejudice, the temperature of their smoldering hatred for him rapidly mounted until their uncontrollable rage was set ablaze.

He reminded them that God had sent the prophet Elijah to a Lebanese widow by the name of Zarephath, who hosted the prophet and obeyed his sayings during the latter part of the drought. God graciously rewarded the Lebanese woman for her hospitality and obedience while Jewish widows starved to death (I Kings 17:9-16). He also pointed out to his reluctant hearers the fact that Naaman, the Syrian captain, was healed from leprosy after obeying the prophet Elisha's advice to "go and wash in the Jordan seven times" (II Kings 5:10). God rewarded the Arabian for taking the prophet's instructions seriously, while Jewish lepers were not healed (II Kings 5:9-14). Naaman returned to thank Elisha and to acknowledge that Jehovah was the only true God (II Kings 5:15).

Here is what the Lord Jesus said:

> But I tell you of a truth, many widows were in Israel in the days of Elias, when the heaven was shut up three years and six months, when great famine was throughout all the land: But unto none of them was Elias sent, save unto Sarepta, a city of Sidon, unto a woman that was a widow. And many lepers were in Israel in the time of Eliseus the prophet; and none of them was cleansed, saving Naaman the Syrian. And all they in the synagogue, when they heard these things, were filled with wrath, And rose up, and thrust him out of the city, and led him unto the brow of the hill . . . that they might cast him down headlong (Luke 4:25-29).

On another occasion, the Lord Jesus withdrew to southern Lebanon for a short period of rest, and a Syrophoenician woman came to him with a very urgent need. (The term Syrophoenician generally refers to the inhabitants of Lebanon living in the proximity of Syria). The woman's daughter had been suffering for some time, "grievously vexed with a devil" (Matthew 15:22). Because of her strong faith in the Lord's ability to heal her afflicted daughter, the woman had searched for him diligently and desperately. When she found him, she "fell at his feet" (Mark 7:25) and pleaded with a broken spirit, saying, "Lord, help me" (Matthew 15:25).

She was aware of the fact that the Jews proudly claimed to be the children of God and that they called the Gentiles dogs. This seems to be the reason she was not surprised when the

Lord spoke in accordance with the predominant Jewish custom: "It is not meet to take the children's bread, and cast it to the dogs" (Matthew 15:26). The Lord may have been testing her faith by referring to the haughty and unfounded superiority complex of the Jews. However, his seemingly harsh expression is softened by the fact that he was pleased with her sincere motive. This is what she said: "Truth, Lord: yet the dogs eat of the crumbs which fall from their masters' table" (Matthew 15:27).

I presume this verse is teaching about the universality of the gospel by implication. Since the Gentiles were called "dogs" by the Jews, and since the Lord Jesus "was made of the seed of David according to the flesh" (Romans 1:3), therefore salvation is freely offered to all true worshipers of the Lord and Savior Jesus Christ. I believe this is what the Lord meant when he said to the Samaritan woman that "salvation is of the Jews" (John 4:22).

With all probability, the Gentiles who were exposed to the teaching of the Hebrew Scriptures were acquainted with Israel's Messianic prophecy concerning the first coming of Christ, and that Christ would come from the seed of David, "out of the town of Bethlehem" (John 7:42; cf. Micah 5:2). God told David, "Of the fruit of thy body will I set upon thy throne" (Psalm 132:11). This truth could be substantiated by the fact that the Samaritans were waiting for the Messiah, "which is called Christ" (John 4:25-30).

Likewise, the Lebanese woman had no problem believing that the Jewish nation was chosen as a vessel for a special reason, and that that reason was fulfilled in the Messiah's first coming. This is what she was mainly concerned with, and she seemed to know that God is neither a Jew nor a Gentile. For this reason, she recognized the Lord as the "son of David," rather than as a Jew (Matthew 15:22). As a result of her unwavering faith, the Lord rewarded her by delivering an evil spirit from her daughter and by giving her a great compliment: "O woman, great is thy faith: be it unto thee even as thou wilt" (Matthew 15:28).

The opening statement of the first chapter of this book is worth repeating here for the purpose of stressing the fact that man is a product of his ethnic heritage, whereby he is conditioned to like and to dislike, to accept and to reject, to love and to hate certain things and certain peoples. Moreover, he has been programmed by his cultural upbringing to interpret and to internalize his acquired beliefs in such a logically deductive manner that God seems to be on his side.

One such interpretation of Scripture is very popular among a multitude of believers in Christ, as well as among unbelievers. It is generally postulated that when God promised to bless Abraham and to curse those who curse him, he was referring to the Jewish nation. It is also commonly asserted by the proponents of this belief that God promised to bless those who would bless the physical Israel and to curse those who would curse the unregenerate Jews. To prove their argument, they feverishly claim that all the nations that were unkind to Israel were punished by God—Babylon, Persia, Greece, Rome, the Arabs, England, Spain, France, Germany, Russia, and many others.

Unfortunately, those who accept this widespread dogma as gospel truth are not only living under the Mosaic law, but also are very fearful of displeasing God by even criticizing Israel for any wrong acts. Such interpretation of Scripture fails to distinguish between the two major doctrines of eschatology and soteriology, and causes confusion and division among the brethren, thus becoming a stumbling block for a great number of believers and unbelievers alike.

Sadly enough, there are many different views on systematic theology, especially when these two important doctrines are discussed. One relates to the absolute necessity of salvation and world evangelization, and the other relates to God's prophetic plan for Israel and the rest of the human race. Soteriology must take precedence over eschatology, mainly because it is directly concerned with the salvation of lost souls. However, it is interesting to note that those who support one view over the other do not even agree on a balanced interpretation of these two doctrines, probably because they tend to follow particular hermeneutical methods based upon their own cultural and ethnic conditioning. For example, some spiritualize and allegorize scriptural truths, while others hold on tenaciously to legalism or literalism in order to remain loyal to their denominational polities and seminary training. Consequently, such unbalanced views cause the Word of God to become "of none effect" through man's tradition and doctrinal persuasion (Mark 7:13).

To top it all off, our Lord and Savior Jesus Christ has been labeled by some as being a biased Jewish God, and his Jewishness has been exploited by many for various reasons. Whether these claims have been utilized by the exploiters advantageously is not of paramount importance to the issue under discussion. Conversely, this kind of promulgation has accomplished at least three things: (1) Since 1948, when God restored Israel as a nation to prepare the world for the great tribulation, the once oppressed Jews have pursued a calculated course of oppressing and antagonizing the native Arab populations; (2) millions of true believers in Christ, and others, proclaim that God is still blessing America, mainly because she is helping the Jews in every possible way; and (3) the vast Arab world, along with other nations, has been greatly provoked to wrath, and their hearts are hardening against the love of God and the gospel of our Lord Jesus Christ, "the Savior of the world" (John 4:42)! Hence, Satan is succeeding in playing havoc with all the offenders and blinding "the minds of them which believe not, lest the light of the glorious gospel of Christ who is the image of God, should shine unto them" (II Corinthians 4:4).

The Call of Abraham

According to Acts 7:2, God called Abraham for the first time while he was still in Mesopotamia. God chose Abraham for three main prophetic reasons: to give the land of Canaan to his physical seed through Isaac; to bless Abraham with great wealth and make him a father of many nations; and to bless the whole human race through Abraham's spiritual seed, the most important promise under discussion. God made Abraham three promises:

> Now the Lord had said unto Abram,* Get thee out of thy country, and from thy kindred, and from thy father's house, unto a land that I will shew thee: And I will make of thee a great nation, and I will bless thee, and make thy name great; and thou shalt be a blessing: And I will bless them that bless thee, and curse him that curseth thee: and in thee shall all families of the earth be blessed (Genesis 12:1-3).

These three promises could comprise possibly the whole spectrum of past, present, and future fulfillments of God's prophetic plan for the human race. The first and second promises and their eschatological and soteriological implications were treated in some detail in the second and third chapters of this book. However, for the purpose of presenting a balanced interpretation, I will briefly summarize their fulfillment, and then I will attempt to clarify the third promise.

It is imperative to state that these three promises cannot possibly be critically explained, for that would be a book in itself. But we do need to investigate some Bible verses and passages, to try to determine whether God's blessing upon Abraham is directly applicable to the Jewish nation.

The aim of this exciting study, therefore, is to gain a balanced interpretation of Genesis 12:3 in particular, in order to establish clear evidence that this blessing is not promised to the physical seed of Abraham, but to the Lord and Savior Jesus Christ, and to the true "Israel of God" (Galatians 3:29, 6:16).

Furthermore, this study is not intended to be conclusive. It is intended rather to stir up inquisitive believers and stimulate them to conduct a more detailed and painstaking research on

---

*Abram means *exalted father;* in Genesis 17:5, his name was changed to Abraham, meaning *a father of many nations.*

such an inspiring issue by totally submitting to the Holy Spirit's reprogramming through his illuminating power, in order that we may be able to unlock controversial scriptural mysteries in a concise and clear manner (I John 2:27). Of course, this must be done for the glory of God and for "the edifying of the body of Christ" (Ephesians 4:12), but also for the sake of all concerned.

Therefore I shall try to present an objective perspective of the three promises made to Abraham, but by doing so, I probably will be likened to the Civil War soldier who put on a Union shirt and Confederate pants and was shot at from all sides.

First Promise

"Now the Lord had said unto Abram, Get thee out of thy country, and from thy kindred, and from thy father's house, unto a land that I will shew thee" (Genesis 12:1).

Abraham was born in Ur around 2165 B.C., and we are told in Joshua 24:2 that his relatives served heathen gods. Although Abraham was trained to worship other gods through the conditioning of his ethnic heritage, God brought him out of darkness and instructed him in the way he should go. Abraham, obeying God without argument, went to Haran, in Syria, before going to Canaan (Palestine). He went first to Haran because there were only two routes to the Promised Land available at that time: across the Arabian desert, which was practically impossible, and along the Euphrates to Haran.

God called Abraham when he was in Iraq and promised him the land of Canaan for a specific reason. While there is some difference of opinion among Bible scholars and historians as to the reason God gave Palestine to the Hebrew nation, the Bible emphatically states that our Lord and Savior Jesus Christ was to be born in that land in the town of Bethlehem (Micah 5:2-5). In other words, the visible manifestation of God in the Incarnation of Christ, through the virgin birth, was necessary not only to render a death blow to Satan at the cross on Calvary, but also to suffer vicariously for our iniquity, in fulfillment of the predictions mentioned in Isaiah 53 concerning the Lord's passion and death. Isaiah tells us that the Lord Jesus will be hated and rejected of men; and that God the Father will bruise his Son and make his soul an offering for sin. First John 2:2 agrees with Isaiah that the Lord Jesus shed his blood for the human race in order to become "the propitiation for our sins: and not for ours only, but also for the sins of the whole world." Only Christ's death as an offering for sin could satisfy God. To say it differently, God's wrath could be satisfied only by the death of Christ (Hebrews 2:17).

The land of Canaan (Palestine) is special to God, and his eyes "are always upon it" (Deuteronomy 11:12). Hosea 9:3 refers to it as "the Lord's land." The Psalmist declares that "the earth is the Lord's, and the fulness thereof; the world and they that dwell therein" (Psalm 24:1). The Bible says that God is the Creator and Owner of the whole universe, and he is at liberty to do with his creation according to his purposes and desires. In fact, he created all things in accordance with his Sovereign will, and for his "pleasure they are and were created" (Revelation 4:11).

I believe God gave Palestine to the Hebrew nation for the following distinct prophetic purposes: (1) to pave the way for the Incarnation of Christ, because his first coming to Palestine forms the golden thread that extends through, and binds together, all the books of the Old Testament into one principal theme, fulfilled at the Cross. Man's redemption through the atoning death of Christ is the most important doctrine of the entire Bible; (2) God has predetermined to punish all unregenerate Jews and Gentiles for rejecting the substitutionary death of Christ by allowing them to go through the great tribulation, "such as was not since the beginning of the world to this time, no, nor ever shall be" (Matthew 24:21). Thus God gave the land of Palestine to the Jews for judgment upon the world. He could have chosen a land other than Palestine and a nation other than Israel, but he did not; and (3) the Lord's millennial reign will take place on the same land so set aside for judgment. The Lord Jesus shall return to rule over all the earth for one thousand years, and his saints will rule with him (Zechariah 14:4-9; Revelation 20:4-6).

Therefore, I am positively persuaded by the Word of God that the Jews as a nation were not chosen for salvation, but were chosen primarily to prepare "a body" for the Messiah (Hebrew 10:5), so that he may save a remnant of Jews and Gentiles (Romans 9:27; Revelation 7:14-17). And since our dear Lord was a Jew according to the flesh, and the Jews were given the privilege of proclaiming "the oracles of God" (Romans 3:2), they were given the first opportunity to hear "the gospel of Christ: for it is the power of God unto salvation to every one that believeth" (Romans 1:16). Hence Christians should not glory in a chosen nation or a chosen land, but should "glory in the Lord" (I Corinthians 1:31; cf. Jeremiah 9:24).

Second Promise

"And I will make of thee a great nation, and I will bless thee, and make thy name great; and thou shalt be a blessing" (Genesis 12:2).

Abraham left his friends and relatives behind in order to obey God's command. God was testing the man by allowing him to renounce the certainties of his past lifestyle and face the uncertainties of the future. Men of God will not mature without a practical knowledge of trial and tribulation. Abraham experienced severe testing during his lifetime, and because of his unwaivering faith, he was called the father of the faithful and friend of God (II Chronicles 20:7; Romans 4:11).

When God called Abraham from Mesopotamia to make him "a father of many nations" (Genesis 17:3-6), he was undoubtedly referring both to the Jews and to their blood relatives, the Arabs and others. God assured Abraham that he would make of him many nations and multiply his physical seed "as the dust of the earth" (Genesis 13:16). Biblically and historically, the Jews have always been small in number, but with the addition of their blood relatives, the Arabs, they have populated the Middle East and other parts of the world for more than four thousand years. They also have been blessed with oil, minerals, and a strategic location.

In an unintended oversight, the story of the Israelites is repeatedly taught in churches and synagogues, while the promises of blessing God made to Hagar and Abraham are totally ignored (Genesis 16:10, 21:13, 18). Abraham's descendants through Isaac are much better known to Christians and Jews than are his descendants through Ishmael and Keturah. The story of Isaac and Rebekah is popular in Jewish and Christian circles, while the consummated marriage of Moses and the Arabian Zipporah is overlooked. More often than not we hear about the Lord Jesus appearing to Abraham, Isaac, and Jacob, but I have never heard a sermon on the thrilling encounter of the Lord Jesus and Hagar (Genesis 16:7). Other than Eve before the Fall, Hagar was probably the only woman in the Old Testament who spoke with God face to face (Genesis 16:7-13). The appearances of God to his people in the Old Testament are called "theophanies." It is my understanding that when the phrase "the angel of the Lord" or "the angel of God" are mentioned in the Old Testament, the article "the" specifically denotes a pre-incarnate appearance of the Lord and Savior Jesus Christ. Furthermore, when Sarah compelled Abraham to "cast out this bondwoman and her son" (Genesis 21:10), God spoke "to Hagar out of heaven" comforting her with the words, "fear not" (Genesis 21:17), and promised to make of Ishmael "a great nation" (Genesis 21:18)!

If God said that he would bless Ishmael and "make him a great nation", (Genesis 17:20), why, then, do we so often hear the opposite? If God said that he loves Arabs as much as he loves Jews and Gentiles, why won't Christians do the same? At any rate, the Bible says that Ishmael, Isaac, and the six sons of Keturah are the physical seed of Abraham from his two wives and a concubine (Genesis 16:15, 21:3, 25:1, 2). God blessed Ishmael and Jacob with exactly the same number of children: He gave both of them twelve sons and one daughter. Ishmael's daughter married Jacob's brother, Esau, who fathered the Edomites, but Jacob's daughter never married.

Moreover, the Moabites and the Ammonites, also Abraham's blood relatives, descended from Lot's two daughters through their sexual relations with their father (Genesis 19:30-38).

In agreement with the Bible, it is obviously clear that the physical descendants of Abraham are not of pure Hebrew lineage, because of blood infusion through intermarriage. For instance, Caleb was a proselyte incorporated into the tribe of Judah. The Moabitess Ruth, the harlot Rahab, the adulteresses Bathsheba and Tamar the Canaanite—all were Gentile women, included in the Messianic line in Matthew 1:3-6 in order to emphasize the universality of the gospel and to stress the inescapable fact that God is neither a Jew nor a Gentile. Furthermore, some of the Arabians and others who were celebrating Pentecost were also proselytized into the various tribes of Israel, and after Peter's powerful sermon, many were converted to Christianity (Acts 2:9-11, 41-47).

With this in mind, it is reasonable to ascertain that when God promised to multiply the seed of Abraham "as the sand which is upon the sea shore" (Genesis 22:17), he was most likely alluding not only to Jews, but also to their blood relatives. Consequently, God has already fulfilled the second promise by multiplying both Arabs and Jews, along with all their blood relatives.

Third Promise

"And I will bless them that bless thee, and curse him that curseth thee: and in thee shall all families of the earth be blessed" (Genesis 12:3).

This is the most important and most misconstrued of God's promises to Abraham. After God had fulfilled the first two promises by making Abraham "very rich in cattle, in silver, and in gold" (Genesis 13:2) and by multiplying his physical seed (Genesis 25), the third promise was fulfilled by the coming of Abraham's seed—Christ (Galatians 3:8, 16). God repeated this particular promise to Abraham (Genesis 22:18); to Isaac (Genesis 26:4); and to Jacob (Genesis 28:14).

Joyfully, we ought to thank our dear Lord for unlocking for

us many controversial spiritual mysteries through the unique ministry of the beloved Apostle Paul. For example, we read that the mystery of the Church, which was unknown in times past, but "by revelation he made known unto me [Paul] the mystery . . . that the Gentiles should be fellow heirs, and of the same body, and partakers of his promise in Christ by the gospel" (Ephesians 3:3-6; cf. Romans 16:25). The mystery spoken of here is that the Jews and Gentiles would be equal heirs in the one Body of Christ. God chose Paul to proclaim the gospel "before the Gentiles, and kings, and the children of Israel" (Acts 9:15).

And now, with the help of the illuminating power of the Holy Spirit, we turn to the unlocking of a most sublime mystery of paramount importance to this study. The doctrine of justification by faith alone has never been expressed in the Bible in a more profound way than in Galatians. It is interesting to note that Paul wrote the Epistle to the Galatians after he was reconditioned by God in the Arabian wilderness (Galatians 1:17). Paul's unswerving commitment to the inerrant and infallible Word of God not only revolutionized the thinking of many religious zealots of his day, but also played a strategic part in the history of the Christian church. The controversy over whether salvation is merited or unmerited was so severe that it shook the early church to its foundation, and kindled the hearts of a number of historians and apologists.

Charles H. Spurgeon once said, "No man can be a true Christian in these days without being a controversialist." It took God at least three years to reprogram Paul's theology so that the Holy Spirit could superintend his spoken and written work. Then Paul became a noble controversialist for his Lord's commission, and "spake boldly in the name of the Lord Jesus, and disputed . . . in the synagogue with the Jews, and with the devout persons, and in the market daily . . . disputing and persuading the things concerning the kindgom of God" (Acts 9:29, 17:17, 19:8).

After the inspired Apostle returned from his wilderness experience, he began to preach and teach a balanced biblical truth of the gospel, in relation to the law and to the promises God made to the Hebrew nation through Abraham. God chose Paul for this unique ministry because he was the only man capable of grasping all that God had decided to teach him. Paul's faith in the Hebrew religion was so intense, and his pharisaic training so exhaustive before his conversion to Christianity, that he went about persecuting the believers, thinking "that he doeth God's service" (John 16:2; cf. Acts 22:3-10).

Exegesis of the Passages

Let us now proceed with our exploratory journey to learn how Paul unlocked the controversial spiritual mystery of Genesis 12:3. He begins his theological argument in chapter 3 of Galatians, with a rebuke, and with sheer surprise that any born-again Christian should turn back from the liberty of the gospel of Christ to the slavery of Judaism. Paul was trying to show the superiority of the gospel over the Mosaic law.

However, the focal point of the argument is disclosed in Galatians 3:7: "Know ye therefore that they which are of faith, the same are the children of Abraham." Paul is saying to the gullible and double-minded Galatian Christians that it is not Abraham's natural descendants, but his spiritual descendants who believe in God for salvation that are his true children. The word *therefore* denotes inference from the passages that precede verse 7. In verse 6, Paul appealed to Genesis 15:6, and in verse 5, he declared that it was by faith that the Holy Spirit had been received by Abraham, and that that was indisputable evidence of sonship (Romans 8:14).

Romans 4:11 asserts that Abraham is "the father of all them that believe, though they be not circumcised; that righteousness might be imputed [transferred] unto them also." It is worth mentioning that Abraham was the first to participate in the rite of circumcision in order to confirm his faith. Paul is trying to help us understand that Abraham's salvation occurred *before* the law was given and the rite of circumcision had been established; that salvation was not by faith *plus* keeping the law, but justification was, and still is, by faith alone (Romans 4:9-25).

The promise God made to Abraham in Genesis 12:3 is a favor, not to be earned or merited by good works. Paul makes it very clear that the seed that will inherit the blessing is not to be equated with those who live under the law, but rather those who share Abraham's faith (Romans 4:16).

The doctrine of justification by faith alone was so abhorrent to the Jews because they could not understand why God should forgive the guilty, let alone justify them by faith. For this and other reasons, they rejected Jesus as the Messiah and utterly disregarded his redemptive plan. However, the doctrine of justification by faith was not something new. The Old Testament confirms that God credits righteousness to those who put their trust in him by faith, and the New Testament shows more clearly that salvation is received by faith (Psalm 37:39; cf. Philippians 3:9).

For this purpose, Paul used Abraham as an example to show that the promise did embody the principles of being declared righteous by believing and trusting God for salvation. Therefore Abraham's faith was credited to him for righteousness (Genesis 15:6; cf. Romans 4:3). In like manner, Peter quoted Genesis 12:3: "And in thy seed shall all the kindreds of the earth be blessed" (Acts 3:25). The words "in thy seed" had all nations in mind and held up Abraham as an example of faith; a like faith is available also to anyone who believes in Jesus Christ of Nazareth, because "neither is there salvation in any other: for there is none other name under heaven given among men, whereby we must be saved" (Acts 4:12).

If one of the greatest minds in history, that of the Apostle Paul, could not fathom "the depth of the riches both of the wisdom and knowledge of God" (Romans 11:33), how then can anyone else explain controversial spiritual mysteries in a logical manner? The only sober way we are able to explain what we do not understand is to humbly agree with God, without adding to or omitting from the Holy Scriptures (Deuteronomy 4:2, 12:32; Proverbs 30:6; Revelation 22:18-19).

The following misconstrued proclamation has become an impediment to the missionaries laboring among some of the one billion Arabs and their counterparts. We often hear that God promised to bless those who bless the physical Israel and curse those who would curse the Jews. The proponents of this belief appeal to Genesis 12:3: "And I will bless them that bless thee, and curse him that curseth thee: and in thee shall all families of the earth be blessed."

Did God say that he would bless those who bless the physical Israel and curse those who would curse the Jews? Of course not! Neither did he promise to bless or curse those who are kind or unkind to the Jews. However, the children of God must not curse anyone, because our dear Lord commanded us: "Love your enemies, bless them that curse you, do good to them that hate you, and pray for them which despitefully use you, and persecute you" (Matthew 5:44). We are to love and pray for the spiritual blessing (salvation) of all the peoples of the earth. Satan and his angels are the only beings that Christians are not commanded to love.

Interestingly enough, I have never heard or read in the Bible about anyone cursing Abraham. On the contrary, Abraham has always been revered by the Arabs, Christians, Jews, and others. But sadly, I have often heard people curse God the Father, God the Son, and use his name in vain without fear (Exodus 20:7).

Moreover, while there is a variety of opinions on the biblical interpretation of Genesis 12:3, the Bible asserts that the point in question does not necessarily apply to Jews, but does refer directly to the Lord and Savior Jesus Christ, and to his spiritual "seed" (I John 3:9; cf. Galatians 3:14). Paul clarifies the problem, in Romans 2:28-29, by arguing that the true Jew is one who has been circumcised spiritually. The Apostle is emphasizing the fact that being Abraham's physical seed does not give all his descendants the right to be called children of God, because Abraham's blessing is passed on only to those who have a like faith. Paul puts to rest this particular argument: "So then they which be of faith are blessed with faithful

Abraham" (Galatians 3:9). On the other hand, all unbelieving Jews and Gentiles are under the curse of God—we understand this by implication from Genesis 12:3.

Certainly God chose Abraham in order that he might bless the believers with eternal salvation through the atoning death of the Lord Jesus (Revelation 5:9), and that he might curse all unregenerate Jews and Gentiles with eternal condemnation (John 5:21-25). The promise of Genesis 12:3, "In thee shall all families of the earth be blessed," is amplified by Genesis 22:18 and repeated in Acts 3:25: "And in thy seed shall all the kindreds of the earth be blessed." The promise was made "till the seed should come" (Galatians 3:19), referring expressly to Abraham's need of a physical heir, through whom the promise of the blessing (salvation), and of the curse (condemnation), should be fulfilled.

At any rate, whatever else is intimated in the promise, the fact remains indisputably clear from the context that it pertains only to a singular seed, "which is Christ" (Galatians 3:16). Obviously, the blessing and cursing by God in Genesis 12:3 apply only to salvation and damnation. We see that the seed mentioned here must be the Lord Jesus and none other (Galatians 3:16). It seems evident in the Lord's Incarnation, his Deity as the Savior, and his finished work at the Cross.

At this time we must ask, how did God preach the gospel of Christ to Abraham? Once more Paul comes to our rescue by unlocking another controversial spiritual mystery: "And the scripture, foreseeing that God would justify the heathen through faith, preached before the gospel unto Abraham, saying, In thee shall all nations be blessed" (Galatians 3:8).

Genesis 3:15 gives us a hint regarding the virgin birth of the Redeemer of mankind two thousand years later. God called Abraham to make him the means by which this prediction could be fulfilled (Genesis 22:18). Similarly, Acts 7:2 instructs us that God had appeared to Abraham long before his salvation took place, mainly because God had decided to bless all the nations of the earth through the Incarnation of the Messiah, so that he might "save sinners" (I Timothy 1:15), rescuing them "from the wrath to come" (Matthew 3:7).

Evidently God preached the gospel of Christ to Abraham and revealed to him the controversial spiritual "mystery of godliness" (I Timothy 3:16). This seems to be the summary of the Incarnation of Christ, his death at the Cross, his burial and resurrection on the third day, and his ascension into heaven (II Timothy 1:10; cf. Acts 1:9-11; I Corinthians 15:1-6). Paul attests to the fact that salvation can be received only by grace through faith, and faith involves knowledge of the gospel of Christ, and knowledge includes acceptance of and adherence to the truth of the gospel (Ephesians 2:8; cf. Romans 10:14). Therefore, since "faith cometh by hearing, and hearing by the word of God" (Romans 10:17), Abraham must have heard the gospel from the precious mouth of the Preincarnate Son of God (Galatians 3:8).

Subsequently, Abraham understood that God would not kill Isaac and that Isaac was a picture-prophecy concerning the death of the only begotten Son of God (Genesis 22:8; cf. Hebrews 11:17-19). The idea of the ram being offered as a substitute for Isaac originated with God in order to illustrate the substitutionary sacrifice of "the Lamb of God, which taketh away the sin of the world" (John 1:29). This exciting illustration is also linked metaphorically to the "Passover lamb" of Exodus 12:11, a breathtaking picture of the finished redemptive work of Christ at Calvary (I Corinthians 5:7)!

Furthermore, many have been also conditioned to believe that God repeated the same promise to Jacob in the following verse of scripture: ". . . cursed be every one that curseth thee, and blessed be he that blesseth thee" (Genesis 27:29).

God did not say that but Isaac did. However, it is difficult to understand how the crafty Rebekah was able to teach her favorite son, Jacob, to lie to his blind father concerning his true identity in order to receive the blessing to the first-born, by resorting to the most contemptible deceit (see Genesis 27:1-29). Jacob even falsely declared that God himself had helped him prepare the meat and bread for Isaac (Genesis 27:20).

The Allegory

Now we come to one of the most unique controversial spiritual mysteries to be found anywhere in the Bible. Unhappily, there are many Christian preachers, and others, who have been treading on dangerous ground by trying to obtain divine approval for their conditioned, or parrot-like, biblical interpretations—concerning Arabs and Jews in particular. For instance, these preachers and their counterparts have been proclaiming that Jews are favored by God over Arabs and others because they are still considered to be his chosen people. To prove their point they make an appeal to the allegory in Galatians 4:22, 24, 30: "Abraham had two sons, the one by a bondmaid, the other by a freewoman. . . . Which things are an *allegory*. . . . Cast out the bondwoman and her son: for the son of the bondwoman shall not be heir with the son of the freewoman" (italics added).

God did not say that Hagar and her son must be thrown out but Sarah did (see Genesis 21:10). Hagar and Ishmael had lived together with Abraham and Sarah for about fifteen years, and Sarah had previously suffered much when Hagar lost respect for her (see Genesis 16:4-6). Now the conflict was renewed when Sarah ". . . saw the son of Hagar . . . mocking" (Genesis 21:9). The Hebrew word "tsâchaq" is an intensive form of the verb on which the word "Isaac" is built. It may be translated as: "mocking," "playing," "sporting," "laughing," and "making sport." There is nothing here to suggest the idea of mocking. I believe Ishmael was playing with his younger brother, as brothers usually do, and Sarah could not bear to see Ishmael sporting with her son as with an equal. Perhaps Sarah may have also feared that Abraham, out of his great love for his first son, would give the older lad the bulk of the inheritance.

Galatians 4:21-31 should not be interpreted literally, because Paul is making an allegorical use of the episode in the history of Ishmael and Isaac to support his argument about the legalistic lifestyle of the religious Jews as opposed to the freedom of the new covenant of grace instituted by Christ. Paul offers a series of contrasts to emphasize the doctrine of justification by faith alone. Hagar and her son are used in reference to the old covenant of the law; Sarah and her son are used to represent the new covenant. The allegory illustrates the danger Christians will face when they are subjected to the covenant of works. However, there is no hidden meaning or anything suggesting that Hagar and Ishmael are rejected by God.

Before going any further, I would like to point out that often a reader may lose the main thought if the setting of the historical account of an allegorical passage is not explained in a narrative form. Following is a very brief version of some absorbing facts regarding the circumstances under which Paul wrote to his Galatian converts.

The Gauls were French barbarians who coerced their way into Greece from western Europe around the third century B.C., and then crossed into Asia Minor (modern Turkey). During the late second century B.C., the region of Galatia became a Roman province under Augustus Caesar.

The Galatians were belligerent but gullible people, easily misled by the superstitions and idolatry of the Romans, and also by Greek mythology. However, like most Gentile heathens of that day, the Galatians were ready to be harvested by the anointed preaching of Paul. The Apostle visited Galatia on his three missionary journeys and planted churches there, as he did in many other places.

Paul earnestly contended "for the faith" and stood adamant against false doctrines (Jude 3). And while Judaizers and others harassed him for more than thirty years during his ministry, he was consumed with passion in the pursuit of preaching the gospel and teaching sound doctrine. The Judaizers followed him from place to place to undermine his labor for Christ (I Corinthians 16:9) and caused him much grief, as the Pharisees and Sadducees had done to the Lord Jesus. Their main mission was to proselytize newly converted Christians, because the Judaizers were fanatic religious Jews who presumably considered Christianity a peculiar sect of Judaism. However, Paul speaks of them as "false brethren" (Galatians 2:4), "grievous wolves," and "false apostles" (Acts 20:28-30; II Corinthians 11:13-15).

These legalistic swindlers were attacking Paul's authenticated apostleship and trying to pervert the gospel of Christ by twisting its meaning in order to justify the dogma that God favors unconverted Jews over Christians and others. Evidently the Galatians were conditioned by such teachings and were attempting to combine their faith in Christ with some legalistic Judaic practices.

In Galatians 4:21-31, Paul delivers a convincing theological argument, beginning with his utter amazement that the Galatian Christians should turn their backs on the liberty of the gospel to return to the slavery of legalism. Paul uses Isaac and Ishmael, in an allegorical form, to emphasize the superiority of salvation by the gospel of Christ over salvation by tediously keeping the law of Moses and the Abrahamic covenant of circumcision. It is obvious that Paul is using the allegory to stress the important fact that salvation "is the gift of God: Not of works, lest any man should boast" (Ephesians 2:8-9). The allegory is a spiritual analogy, or illustration, of the old covenant of law with Israel and the new covenant of grace (salvation) with the Church of God.

The dictionary defines allegory as "figurative treatment of one subject under the guise of another . . . a symbolic narrative . . . to speak as to imply something other." Paul is using this method to interpret a literal text in a more profound spiritual sense; we must use this same method in interpreting Galatians 4:21-31. It is bewildering that so many Bible scholars and others have been trying, willingly or unwillingly, to twist the true meaning of this particular passage in order to further their theological persuasion. By misinterpreting such controversial spiritual mysteries, the Scripture ceases to be the basic authority, and the interpreter becomes the mouth of God. Once an individual departs from the Holy Spirit's guidance in the plain meaning of Scripture, the reader is exposed to the conditioned understanding of the human interpreter.

It is interesting to note that the word *allegory* was used in the plenary inspired Word of God only once, in Galatians 4:24. Perhaps the Holy Spirit desired to intimidate Paul's adversaries, who were spreading a Judaistic theology among the newly formed churches, or simply wanted to confound the wise. But whatever view we take of Galatians 4:21-31 is immaterial to the fact that the Jews of the old Abrahamic covenant are no longer the chosen people of God. But they do remain his chosen prophetic time clock.

Since the word *allegory* was never used before or after Galatians 4:24, its usage here is undoubtedly intended to ascertain that all believers in Christ are the only chosen people unto salvation. At the expense of being redundant, Paul argues, using the spiral method of learning, that the two sons of Abraham, the bondwoman and the freewoman, the two covenants, and the two Jerusalems—all these illustrate the fact that the chosen people of God are "the children of God by faith in Christ Jesus. . . . There is neither Jew nor Greek . . . and if ye be Christ's, then are ye Abraham's seed, and heirs according to the promise" (Galatians 3:26, 28-29)!

In other words, Ishmael and Isaac, Sarah and Hagar, the covenant of law and the covenant of grace, the earthly Jerusalem and the heavenly Jerusalem—all are analogous to eternal salvation as opposed to eternal damnation. Paul is simply saying that an individual can either be justified by faith in Christ Jesus, or be condemned for rejecting the Savior. When the orthodox Jews sought to kill the Messiah for claiming to be Yahweh, the Lord stated that they were not the true seed of Abraham, that their father was not God, but the "devil." In fact, the Bible identifies Satan as the father of all unbelieving Jews and Gentiles (John 8:39-44; cf. I John 3:8-10).

Therefore the chosen people of God are only those who "are led by the Spirit of God . . . the children of God. . . . According as he hath chosen us in him before the foundation of the world . . . a chosen generation . . . are now the people of God" (Romans 8:14, 16; Ephesians 1:4; I Peter 2:9-10). Hence, the chosen people of God are those who belong to God's family. The Lord Jesus calls them "my brother, and my sister, and mother . . . these my brethren" (Mark 3:35; Matthew 25:40; II Corinthians 6:14-18). Finally, Paul puts to rest this wearisome argument by affirming that the saints of God are "the household of God . . . And . . . the Israel of God" (Ephesians 2:19; Galatians 6:16)!

Conversely, Israel's special election as God's covenant people was rooted in divine love from beginning to end, and the grounds for the choice lay utterly in God alone and not in any good deeds or credits the nation had accumulated. It is obvious that the purpose behind Israel's election was to fulfill God's prophetic plan of redemption. Therefore, in choosing the Jews God did establish a beachhead in human history from which all nations would acknowledge his sovereignty and submit totally to his will (Genesis 12:1-3: Cf. Phillippians 2:9-11).

We have already seen that Genesis 12:3 and the allegory of Galatians 4:21-31 may very well be the most misconstrued and abused scriptures in the entire Bible, and this is not a reflection on the Bible itself. Rather this misuse and abuse attest to the flagrancy and perversity of man's total depravity. Undoubtedly, all of us have been conditioned to search subjectively for certain things that seem to put God on our side. Hence, at times, we are entirely too prone to clothe our sins in the garments of sanctity by appealing to the Bible!

Chapter Five
Life Is the Blood

The human body consists of many different kinds of fixed and complex elements, but the blood is the only mobile element that contributes much to the life of the body. In fact, there can be no life without it. Unlike the other elements, the blood is a fluid that is pumped by the heart and circulates throughout the entire body in about twenty-five seconds. The cells are constantly nourished and cleansed by it; the moment it fails to reach them, they die. The blood circulates through the arteries and capillaries, carrying oxygen and nutrients to all parts of the body and disposing of carbon dioxide and other wastes in a breathtaking process called metabolism. The colorless fluid of the blood, the plasma, contains a variety of cells and substances. The red cells, which number approximately five million per cubic millimeter and give the blood its red color, carry out the rhythmic exchange of oxygen and carbon dioxide between the lungs and the body tissues. There are also white cells, whose main function is to defend the body against infection and foreign agents. The normal human body contains about six quarts of blood, and every cubic millimeter has between five and ten thousand white cells; their number increases in the presence of infection. Although the analysis of blood applies also to the animal kingdom, my primary interest here is to discuss the reason God instituted the rite of blood sacrifice.

Mystery of the Blood

The case in point illustrates that the blood is the most important of all the parts of the human body, because there can be no life without it. I believe God commanded Moses concerning the necessity of blood sacrifice because it has to do with the mystery of life. Leviticus 17:11 reads as follows: "For the life of the flesh is in the blood: and I have given it to you upon the altar to make an atonement for your souls: for it is the blood that maketh an atonement for the soul." This same inspired truth is repeated in the verse 14: *"For the life of all flesh is the blood"* (italics added.)

The Bible is a book of blood, circulating from Genesis through Revelation. God instituted the doctrine of blood sacrifice in the Old Testament for two specific reasons: (1) The life of the body originates from it; and (2) it is the means by which atonement is achieved. Atonement is an Old Testament term meaning *to cover,* or *to put sin out of sight.* Literally, atonement means *reconciliation.* Man could be reconciled to God, or elevated to his moral perfection, only by Christ's substitutionary blood sacrifice at the Cross on Calvary.

Now let us discuss the reason God required the rite of blood sacrifice. Genesis 2:7 declares, "And the *Lord* God formed man of the dust of the ground, and breathed into his nostrils the breath of life; and man became a living soul"! Adam's body was formed from the elements of the earth, but his blood was a gift of God. The body was a lump of matter without life, but when God added pure blood to that body and breathed into it the breath of life, the breath of God ignited the circulation of the blood and Adam became a living soul. In fact, the name Adam means just that. The syllable A is the first letter of the alphabet, indicating that the Lord God is the beginning of all things, for the Bible asserts that the Lord Jesus is the "Alpha, and Omega, the beginning and the ending" (Revelation 1:8). Alpha and Omega are the first and last letters of the Greek alphabet, symbolizing that the Lord Jesus is the Creator and Judge of all things. Both the Hebrew word *dam* (pronounced dawm) and the Arabic word *dem* mean *blood.* Therefore the name Adam means *blood from God.*

Since the life of the human body originates from the blood, and since the blood is the only means by which atonement is made, something dreadful happened to the blood the moment Adam disobeyed God in the Garden of Eden. God created Adam with the ability not to sin, but when he did sin, sin entered his bloodstream and was transmitted to all his posterity; because God has made of Adam's "blood all nations of men for to dwell on all the face of the earth" (Acts 17:26). Apart from what the Bible tells us about the doctrine of blood sacrifice, no one would be able to fathom the mystery of God's love for the fallen human race. In view of the fact that Adam's sin of disobedience caused "blood poisoning" and resulted in death, and since God had determined to save sinners from his future wrath through the atoning death of his only begotten Son, the virgin birth and the death of Christ were indispensable. The Lord Jesus affirms this truth: "For the Son of man is come to seek and to save that which was lost. . . . This cup is the new testament in my blood, which is shed for you" (Luke 19:10, cf. 22:20).

New Testament literally means New Covenant. The word Covenant is an Old Testament term meaning an agreement between two parties. The covenant of the Old Testament was restricted to God's dealings with Israel, while the covenant of the New Testament concerns God's dealing with man's salvation through faith in the substitutionary shed blood of Christ on the cross, the central theme of the entire New Testament.

Redemption is accomplished *only* by the power of the blood of the Lord and Savior Jesus Christ. The Bible says, "Neither by the blood of goats and calves, but by his own blood he . . . obtained eternal redemption for us" (Hebrews 9:12). "Redemption" means that Christ paid the price to set sinners free from the wrath of God and from the bondage of sin. The Lord Jesus offered the free gift of eternal salvation to all who "eat the flesh of the Son of man, and drink his blood. . . . He that eateth of this bread shall live forever" (John 6:53, 58). In other words, just as it is needful for man to eat bread and drink water in order to sustain physical life, so it is also necessary to appropriate Christ's atoning death in order to receive the free gift of eternal life. God could have chosen another means to justify sinful men, but he did not. He wanted to demonstrate his unspeakable love for the human race, and thus decided to redeem us by his own blood (Revelation 1:5); because, as the Lord Jesus graciously stated, "Greater love hath no man than this, that a man lay down his life for his friends" (John 15:13).

The angels never have been able to comprehend the unspeakable love of God, because he did not plan to provide redemption for them. If it had not been for Adam's sinful nature, the saints of God would never have been able to comprehend, with the help of the illuminating power of the blessed Holy Spirit, "the breadth, and length, and depth, and height" of God's love in Christ Jesus (Ephesians 3:18). Again God used Paul to unlock another controversial spiritual mystery, this time by contrasting man's total depravity and death in Adam with eternal life in Christ:

> Wherefore, as by one man sin entered into the world, and death by sin; and so death passed upon all men, for that all have sinned. . . . For the wages of sin is death; but the gift of God is eternal life through Jesus Christ our Lord (Romans 5:12, 6:23).

Paul is actually saying that if Adam's sin resulted in death, how much more will Christ's redemptive work reconcile man to God. Since "the life of the flesh is in the blood," so the death of the flesh is in the blood also, "and as it is appointed unto men once to die . . . so Christ was once offered to bear the sins of many" (Hebrews 9:27-28).

Of course, this does not mean that all the peoples of the world will be saved from the wrath of God. To be saved they must personally receive the free gift of grace and appropriate the righteousness that God makes available through the vicarious death of Christ. True believers can assuredly declare that we have been "justified by his blood, we shall be saved from wrath through him" (Romans 5:9). This assurance of salvation is given only to those who are rejoicing "in God through our Lord Jesus Christ, by whom we have now received the atonement" (Romans 5:11). This is the only time the word *atonement* is used in the New Testament.

The universality of sin and death come to all men—not because they live a sinful life, but because they have inherited Adam's sinful blood—for God "hath made of one blood all nations of men" (Acts 17:26). For this reason Adam's sin was imputed (transmitted via the blood) to his posterity. In other words, from Adam's time until the Great White Throne judgment, all unsaved Jews and Gentiles will be judged and condemned by the Lord Jesus Christ because of their total depravity inherited from Adam.

The Virgin Birth

The Bible teaches clearly that the Lord and Savior Jesus Christ was conceived in the womb of the virgin Mary by a supernatural act of the Holy Ghost:

> Now the birth of Jesus Christ was on this wise: When as his mother Mary was espoused to Joseph, before they came together, she was found with child of the Holy Ghost. . . . For that which is conceived in her is of the Holy Ghost . . . and they shall call his name Emmanuel, which being interpreted is, God with us (Matthew 1:18, 20, 23; cf. Isaiah 7:14).

And Luke tells us that

> The angel Gabriel was sent from God . . . to a virgin . . . and the virgin's name was Mary. . . . And the angel said unto her . . . behold, thou shalt conceive in thy womb, and bring forth a son, and shalt call his name JESUS. He shall be great, and shall be called the Son of the Highest. . . . The Holy Ghost shall come upon thee, and the power of the Highest

shall overshadow thee: therefore also that holy thing which shall be born of thee shall be called the Son of God (Luke 1:26-27, 30-32, 35).

The blood poisoning which was transmitted from Adam to his posterity necessitated the virgin birth of Christ. God could have chosen any other means to reconcile fallen men unto himself, but in view of God's righteous demands for judgment on the sinner, *only* the precious blood of the Lord Jesus was sufficient to pay the penalty for our sins, "and not for ours only, but also for the sins of the whole world" (I John 2:2).

Ever since sin entered the blood of man, the matter of man's reconciliation to God has been the most important of all questions. The first revelation of God's answer to that question was his prediction that the offspring of the woman would crush the head of the serpent (Genesis 3:15). This was the first prediction concerning the Incarnation and death of the Lord and Savior Jesus Christ. The blood sacrifice of the firstborn was instituted by God when he provided "coats of skins" to clothe Adam and Eve after the Fall (Genesis 3:21). Man's fellowship with God can be restored *only* by the shedding of blood.

God accepted Abel's sacrifice of the firstborn of his flock but rejected Cain's offering of his best fruit (Genesis 4:3-5). However, what the millions of animals sacrificed since the time of Adam could not accomplish, the shed blood of the Lord Jesus Christ provided, so that sinful men could be reconciled to God. Man cannot find favor with God and be "redeemed with corruptible things, as silver and gold . . . but with the precious blood of Christ, as of a lamb without blemish and without spot" (I Peter 1:18-19).

God said that "the life of the flesh is in the blood; and . . . it is the blood that maketh an atonement for the soul. . . . Therefore . . . the life of all flesh is the blood" (Leviticus 17:11, 14). Since Adam was the federal head of the human race, and since his sinful blood is circulating in the veins of his posterity, man will remain subject to the curse of death and eternal separation from God. The Bible says, "And as it is appointed unto men once to die, but after this the judgment" (Hebrews 9:27). However, our dear Lord dealt with sin once and for all through the shedding of his blood, because "without shedding of blood is no remission. . . . So Christ was once offered to bear the sins of many; and unto them that look for him shall he appear the second time" (Hebrews 9:22, 28). When the Lord returns from heaven at the consummation of the age, he will take redeemed sinners to himself and judge all unbelieving Jews and Gentiles for rejecting his blood sacrifice. A willful rejection of his sacrifice is final and unforgivable. John the Baptizer clarifies this doctrine in the following truth: "Behold the Lamb of God, which taketh away the sin of the world. . . . He that believeth on the Son hath everlasting life; and he that believeth not the Son shall not see life; but the wrath of God abideth on him" (John 1:29, 3:36).

The supernatural conception by the Holy Ghost was the *only* way the virgin birth could be accomplished. Mary presented her body so that Christ could come to earth in a visible human form in order to pay the price for sin. Quoting Psalm 40:6-8, the book of Hebrews confirms this truth:

> For it is not possible that the blood of bulls and of goats should take away sins. Wherefore when [Christ] cometh into the world, he saith, Sacrifice and offering thou wouldest not, *but a body hast thou prepared me:* In burnt offerings and sacrifices for sin thou hast had no pleasure. . . . We are sanctified through the offering of the body of Jesus Christ once for all (Hebrews 10:4-6, 10, italics added).

The finality of Christ's redemptive work on the Cross satisfied the holy nature and character of God concerning the penalty for sin. For this specific reason, Mary was chosen to provide the vehicle for the Lord's body, without the help of a human father. Mary had nothing to do with the conception, the Holy Spirit being solely responsible for the miracle of the conception of the body of Christ. After conception, the blood of Christ never came into direct contact with the blood of

Mary. This fact is well established scientifically. Oxygen and nutrients are exchanged from mother to baby through the placenta, with the two bloods never touching. The foetal and maternal blood are separated from each other by the walls of the foetal blood vessels, and there is no actual mingling of the two blood currents. In other words, no foetal blood ever flows to the mother, nor is there any direct maternal blood-flow to the foetus. Therefore, the blood of Christ was protected from inheriting or touching his mother's sinful blood. The flesh came from a Jewish virgin named Mary, but Christ is begotten of God. The word *begotten* signifies blood connection. The divine blood of Christ came from God, because the Lord Jesus is from the same substance as God, and also has the same attributes and characteristics as God in his Deity. God the Father identifies Christ as the eternal God the Son, the Creator and Owner of all things:

> Thou art my son, this day have I begotten thee. . . . Unto the Son he saith, Thy throne, *O God,* is for ever and ever. . . . Thou, Lord, in the beginning hast laid the foundation of the earth; and the heavens are the works of thine hands; They shall perish; but thou remainest (Hebrews 1:5, 8, 10-11; cf. Colossians 1:15-20).

The Old Testament stated that the eternal Son of God must come in human form (Incarnation) to pay the price demanded by our Holy God for our deliverance from sin. The shedding of blood required physical human flesh, so that the incorruptible blood of Christ could set sinners free from the penalty of death. The Bible affirms this truth by stating that God came in a human body, "to give his life a ransom for many" (Mark 10:45); that "through death he might destroy . . . the power of death . . . and deliver them who through fear of death were all their lifetime subject to bondage. . . . He took on him the seed of Abraham . . . to make reconciliation [atonement] for the sins of the people" (Hebrews 2:14-17; cf. I John 4:1-3).

The sin of Adam interrupted normal relations between God

and man. Sin corrupted the blood of men and resulted in death and eternal separation from fellowship with God. However, in order to restore peace and fellowship with God, sinless and incorruptible blood was needed. *Only* the supernatural blood of Christ could satisfy God's requirement for justice. The Bible says, "Christ died for the ungodly. . . . Being now justified by his blood, we shall be saved from wrath. . . . We were reconciled to God by the death of his Son . . . by whom we have now received the atonement" (Romans 5:6, 9-11).

The body of Christ came from a Jewish mother, but the blood of the eternal Son of God was of the Holy Spirit. The body of Christ can save no one, but in order that God may save sinners, it was necessary for him to come in Jewish flesh, as predicted. At the moment of conception, the power of God "overshadowed the womb of Mary," and protected Christ from inheriting his mother's sin-nature. This supernatural creative act is a miracle of the blessed Holy Spirit; "for with God nothing shall be impossible" (Luke 1:35, 37)! Therefore, God the Son did not have a mother. The Virgin Mary is the mother of Jesus in his humanity, because she bore the body of the Incarnate Son of God. This seems to be the reason the Lord Jesus called himself "the Son of man" (Matthew 18:11).

God is not a Jew

Paul outlines the reason for the Incarnation and resurrection of Christ: "Great is the mystery of godliness: God was manifest in the flesh . . . preached unto the Gentiles, believed on in the world, received up into glory" (I Timothy 3:16). This is a summary of the entire Messianic work of Christ. In like manner, the Lord Jesus magnified the truth by unveiling this great controversial spiritual mystery to a woman of Samaria. The Samaritans were of mixed Jewish and Gentile blood through intermarriage; thus they probably were conditioned to believe that salvation came from the Jews and that God must be worshiped in a synagogue or a temple. This is what the Lord said:

Woman, believe me, the hour cometh, when ye

shall neither in this mountain, nor yet at Jerusalem, worship the Father. Ye worship ye know not what: we know what we worship: for salvation is of the Jews. But the hour cometh, and now is, when the true worshippers shall worship the Father in spirit and in truth: for the Father seeketh such to worship him. God is Spirit: and they that worship him must worship him in spirit and in truth (John 4:21-24).

What a priceless revelation this is, and will ever remain, to all true worshipers of the Lord Jesus. This may be called the heavenly Emancipation Proclamation. Christ came to set sinners free from the curse of sin and death, and also from all prescribed procedures of public worship. The Lord God came in the flesh for this very reason; "if the Son therefore shall make you free, ye shall be free indeed" (John 8:36). This does not mean that a true born-again Christian should not worship the Lord in a local church; on the contrary, the Bible exhorts believers not to forsake "the assembling of ourselves together, as the manner of some is; but exhorting one another: and so much more, as ye see the day approaching" (Hebrews 10:25). However, to probe further into the mystery of salvation and true worship of God, we need to understand what the Lord Jesus meant in his discourse with the Samaritan woman.

When the Lord Jesus told her that "salvation is of the Jews," I believe he was wondering whether her dislike of Jews would hinder her from accepting the fact that God the Savior came in Jewish flesh. The Lord tested her faith, just as he had tested that of the Syrophoenician woman (Matthew 15:26-28).

To paraphrase Martin Luther's analogy of faith, Scripture must be diligently compared with Scripture in order to arrive at a proper understanding of truth. With this in mind, let us try to unlock another sublime spiritual mystery, with the help of the illuminating power of the blessed Holy Spirit.

Long before the creation of the world, the eternal Son of God knew that he would meet and save a sinful Samaritan woman. However, he also was well aware that Jews and Samaritans hated one another with passion. The Jews cursed and rejected the Samaritans for their mixed blood and their different religious customs; the Samaritans reciprocated that hate and did not mingle with Jews. For instance, when the Lord Jesus was passing with his disciples through a Samaritan village, the Samaritans refused them lodging. As a result of this mutual dislike, James and John wanted to call down fire from heaven to destroy the inhabitants, but the Lord Jesus rebuked the disciples for their ethnic pride and prejudice (Luke 9:51-56).

The seed of hate between the two peoples had begun to germinate long after the fall of Samaria to Assyria, around 721 B.C. The Assyrians intermarried with Israelites, and their offspring became known as Samaritans. Samaria was the capital of the northern kingdom (the ten tribes of Israel) and the center of idolatry. King Ahab and his wicked Lebanese queen, Jezebel, had built a temple there and worshiped Baal. God sent the prophets Elijah and Elisha to preach against idolatry, but most of their warnings were ignored.

Conversely, it is interesting to note that the Samaritans were familiar with the Hebrew Scriptures and were anxiously awaiting the first coming of the Messiah, "which is called Christ . . . the Saviour of the world" (John 4:25, 42). They recognized only the Pentateuch and were more scrupulous about observing its ordinances than were the orthodox Jews. For example, instead of worshiping God at Jerusalem and compromising with the prescribed procedures of public worship, they had built a beautiful temple on Mount Gerizim (near modern Nablus), where they worshiped in accordance with their own established religious customs.

The Lord Jesus chose a woman living in adultery in order to teach us that God is neither a Jew nor a Gentile. Only God can do what appears to be a foolish thing; the Bible declares that "God hath chosen the foolish things of the world to confound the wise; and God hath chosen the weak things of the world to confound the things which are mighty; And base things of the world, and things which are despised, hath God chosen" (I Corinthians 1:27-28).

Shortly after healing blind Bartimaeus and saving him, along with Zacchaeus, at Jericho, the Lord Jesus went up the hills to Jerusalem, then walked more than thirty miles to keep his divine rendezvous at Jacob's well in Sychar (near Nablus). After all, that was the main reason Almighty God himself came to sinful humanity in the Incarnation (John 1:14; cf. Philippians 2:6). The visible manifestation of God in Christ may be called the God-man. God became human, without the sin-nature (II Corinthians 5:21), so that he might be able "to seek and to save that which was lost" (Luke 19:10).

The Bible says that "no man hath seen God at any time" (John 1:18; I John 4:12). The Lord Jesus revealed this controversial spiritual mystery to the Samaritan woman, saying that no man has ever seen God in his essence because "God is Spirit" (John 4:24). Since God is Spirit, and only he could be an adequate Savior, God assumed visible human flesh in order to make his death and the shedding of his precious royal blood effective, once for all, as a payment for sin (Hebrews 10:10). In other words, the body that God had prepared for himself through the Virgin Mary could save no man (Hebrews 10:5). For this reason God became human—to be able to suffer and die for the redemption of sinners "out of every kindred, and tongue, and people, and nation" (Revelation 5:9). Therefore, God is neither a Jew nor a Gentile; "God is Spirit: and they that worship him must worship him in spirit and in truth" (John 4:24)!

The Impeccability of Christ

The doctrine that Christ was not able to sin when he was tempted is designated by the term *impeccability.* The impeccability of Christ is an absolute prerequisite to his substitutionary death on the Cross. However, some orthodox theologians maintain that Christ could have sinned if he had wished, but did not, even under the greatest provocation. These theologians argue that it is difficult to fathom how his temptations could have been genuine, if he could not sin.

Many times when I am trying to persuade my Muslim friends of their total depravity through the doctrine of the blood, and of their imperative need for salvation, they lose no time in pointing out that if Christ could have sinned when tempted, why should they accept such an imperfect Savior? And if Christ really claimed to be God in the flesh, how could he succumb to inferior worldly forces? Furthermore, when Christians try to justify their human weakness by implying that Christ was capable of sin, don't they know they are promoting the propagation of Islam? My Muslim friends discussed these and other things with me and tried in vain to discourage and proselytize me.

These questions raised by the Muslims are very real and challenging. Unfortunately, a multitude of evangelical Christians have been conditioned to believe that our dear Lord and Savior Jesus Christ could have sinned, because he was a true man. To justify their argument, they appeal to the only Bible verse that seems to give a claim to their belief: "For we have not an high priest which cannot be touched with the feeling of our infirmities; but was in all points tempted like as we are, yet without sin" (Hebrews 4:15). Part of their problem lies in not discerning what the verse says and what it does not say. The verse does not say that Christ was tempted with a view to proving that he could sin. He was tested in order to prove he was sinless, because he did not have a sin-nature as we do. The words "tempted like as we are" signify that the Lord Jesus was a true man, but was not capable of sin (Romans 8:3).

To ascertain whether Christ could have sinned due to the presence of a human nature, we should examine very briefly the character of temptation.

We must remember that Christ was not only perfect man, but also perfect God, "for in him dwelleth all the fullness of the God-head bodily" (Colossians 2:9). This statement affirms both the Deity and the humanity of the Lord Jesus, the God-Man. God took upon himself human limitations by adding a human nature to his divine nature. These two natures were united in One Person without mixture (John 17:5). As a man he humbled himself and submitted to diverse human sufferings, becoming "obedient unto death, even the death of the cross", without giving up any attributes of his Deity. In other words, the eternal Son of God condescended to become man by the voluntary waiving of some of his divine privileges, and by veiling his glory in order to be able to accomplish his redemptive work (Philippians 2:5-11).

Hence the God-Man was not susceptible to sin, because of his holy nature and holy character. The translation of the word *tempted* from the Greek, literally means to *test, try,* and *solicit to evil.* The Bible says:

> Blessed is the man that endureth temptation: for when he is tried, he shall receive the crown of life, which the Lord hath promised to them that love him. Let no man say when he is tempted, I am tempted of God: *for God cannot be tempted with evil,* neither tempteth he any man: But every man is tempted, when he is drawn away of his own lust, and enticed (James 1:12-14, italics added).

The Lord's temptation in the wilderness after forty days of fasting was a trial no other human has experienced, or will ever experience. However, his greatest temptation took place in the garden of Gethsemane, before the excruciating pain on the cross. The Bible says that Christ does "always those things that please" the Father (John 8:29). It is evident that his human will never acted independently from his divine will. This should be proof of the impeccability of Christ, because the divine will of God cannot sin.

It is worth noting that the temptation of our Lord Jesus does not convey the idea of luring him into sin, but has in view the inner personal suffering that results from external trials and adversities. James refutes the speculation that God could be tempted with evil, insisting that God cannot be tested in the same manner as sinful men. His temptation was that of suffering and was not connected with the lust of the flesh.

We have seen already that our dear Lord not only went through similar "feeling of our infirmities," but also suffered under the most grueling circumstances, much more than any man can bear. It is true that he took the likeness of sinful flesh and blood (Hebrews 2:14), but it is also true that his blood is sinless. Since our sin-nature is an outgrowth of sin transmitted through the blood, and since the blood of Christ is sinless, therefore Christ was not capable of sin!

The Body of Christ

The ugly fact is that several hundred million Arabs and their counterparts appear to disrespect and distrust Christian missionaries, mainly because most Christians have been conditioned to believe that the Almighty favors Israel over all other nations; that God the Savior is a Jew; that God will curse those who curse Israel; that the Jews are still the chosen people; that the Lord Jesus was capable of sinning in the same manner we do, in spite of his claims to be God in the flesh; and that the Church of the Lord Jesus consists of man-made denominations. These are some of the promulgations that Arabs and others abhor.

I have already discussed the biblical view of these impediments to evangelizing Arabs and others, except for denominationalism. The New Testament teaches that there are only two kinds of churches: (1) the local church; and (2) the universal Church. The local church is seen in local assemblies that have been redeemed by the shed blood of the Lord and Savior Jesus Christ. On the other hand, the universal Church is comprised of all the redeemed. However, the true Church does not have a hierarchy of any kind, because this very thing is condemned by our Lord, particularly in the seven churches of Revelation's second and third chapters. Our Master did not subscribe to the practice of an honored priesthood and a lesser laity within a local assembly. On the contrary, he preferred the plain and humble people who gave him his rightful place in their worship services, rather than stressing bureaucratic religious public worship.

Christians from the various man-made denominations seem to be confused about the true meaning of the Church. More often than not, they identify it with a building where people meet for a variety of religious activities. Not only that, Christians are divided among themselves on many unimportant matters, while people are perishing without hope for eternal life. To top it all off, Christians are preoccupied with their church business meetings, activities, and government, not heeding the Lord's command to go "into all the world, and preach the gospel to every creature" (Mark 16:15; cf. Matthew 28:18-20).

Following is a brief background of the meaning of the word *church*. The etymological meaning in the Greek is *ekklesia*, made up of two words from the verb *ekkaleo: ek*, meaning *out;* and *kaleo, to call or summon*. The two words together mean *to call out*. However, in New Testament secular Greek, *ekklesia* signified an assembly hall or meeting place, where people gathered to discuss or debate social or political issues (Acts 19:32, 39, 41). The same word was used in the Septuagint to denote a gathering of people for almost any type of activity. Later on, the disciples of Christ interpreted the word as applying to believers assembled together to worship the Lord and Savior Jesus Christ and to fellowship. And then *ekklesia* became known as the Church of the Lord Jesus, whether believers assemble together or not (Acts 8:1-3).

The Church is also known as the Body of Christ. This was a hidden spiritual mystery "which from the beginning of the world hath been hid in God" (Ephesians 3:9). Paul defines this sublime mystery in Ephesians 3:6: "That the Gentiles should be fellowheirs, and of the same body, and partakers of his promise in Christ by the gospel." The Jews of the New Testament seemed to believe that God still favored them over the Gentiles, but the Bible teaches the opposite. The mystery here concerns the Gentiles and consists of their equal spiritual position and privilege in Christ by means of the gospel. This equality and privilege are described in this way: "fellowheirs," "fellow-members of the same body of Christ," "fellow-partakers of eternal life." Paul is saying that only regenerated Jews and Gentiles are able to share equal spiritual blessing. To say it differently, the Body of Christ is comprised of Jews and Gentiles who are baptized by the Holy Spirit at the very moment of salvation. First Corinthians 12:13 asserts that the prime requisite for entrance into the Body of Christ is baptism of the Holy Spirit. Romans 8:9 supports this truth: "Now if any man have not the Spirit of Christ, he is none of his." Therefore, the Body of Christ is an organism, not an organization. It is true that the Body of Christ is universal, but it is visible in the believers making up the local assemblies.

As all men are related by the sinful blood of Adam, and this blood carries the sentence of eternal death; so the members of the Body of Christ are related by his sinless blood, and his precious blood gives us eternal life. We have already seen that there can be no physical life without blood, because "the life of the flesh is in the blood" (Leviticus 17:11). Likewise, there can be no reconciliation between God and man without the shed blood of "our Lord Jesus Christ, by whom we have now received the atonement" (Romans 5:11). And although un-believing members in the local churches do not belong to the Body of Christ (Matthew 7:21), the universal Church—to which every true believer belongs—depends solely upon the blood of Christ for cleansing, nourishment, and growth. These three terms need to be explained briefly in order to com-prehend what takes place after salvation.

Cleansing

Every part of the human body must be constantly cleansed by the circulation of the blood. Otherwise foreign matter and waste products will invade the body and render it inoperative. In like manner, every member in the Body of Christ must be regularly cleansed by his blood. Regenerated sinners should confess and try to forsake their sinful habits in order to be protected against Satanic obstructions and be able to commu-nicate with God through prayers that may be answered, because "The effectual fervent prayer of a righteous man availeth much" (James 5:16).

The majority of believers are not perturbed by their daily prayerless lifestyle. Some of my Christian friends have told me on numerous occasions that "since God is blessing us richly without the legalistic view of agonizing in prayer, why should we not be content with God's blessings?" I am reminded that God "maketh his sun to rise on the evil and the good, and sendeth rain on the just and on the unjust" (Matthew 5:45); and "He is kind unto the unthankful and to the evil" (Luke 6:35). Our loving Lord who gives breath to the murderer and food to those who curse and reject him—that same God will never forsake his children, even though they do not pray and confess their daily sins (Hebrews 13:5). However, because confession is commanded by God for daily victorious living and cleansing, we need to confess and forsake the sins God hates. When we confess our iniquity with a repentant heart, God promises to "forgive us our sins, and to cleanse us from all unrighteousness . . . in his own blood" (I John 1:7-9; Revelation 1:5)!

Nourishment

Beside cleansing, the blood nourishes the human body by transporting various types of nutrients and oxygen, thus generating life and vitality in the entire body. Although our physical nourishment is ephemeral, spiritual nourishment is much more important, and its reward has eternal value.

For forty years, the Lord God fed Israel manna in the wilderness. And the Jews saw him feed more than five thousand—a miracle similar to their wilderness experience—but that kind of bread was for temporary physical sustenance. The manna that came from heaven represented Christ. A statement from our Lord is worth repeating for the purpose of clarifying the meaning of eating the flesh of Christ and drinking his blood:

> Verily, verily, I say unto you, Except ye eat the flesh of
> the Son of man, and drink his blood, ye have no life
> in you. Whoso eateth my flesh, and drinketh my

blood, hath eternal life; and I will raise him up at the last day. For my flesh is meat indeed, and my blood is drink indeed. He that eateth my flesh, and drinketh my blood, dwelleth in me, and I in him. As the living Father hath sent me, and I live by the Father: so he that eateth me, even he shall live by me. This is that bread which came down from heaven: not as your fathers did eat manna, and are dead: he that eateth of this bread shall live for ever (John 6:53-58).

This seemingly harsh saying, referring to the Lord's death and ascension, which would confirm his Deity and saving power, has been misconstrued by Jews and Gentiles alike. In view of the Old Testament warning against the consumption of blood (Leviticus 7:26-27), the Lord's words offended the Jews. Conversely, Catholics have been conditioned to believe that the bread and wine become the actual flesh and blood of Christ; that at the moment of consumption, this Eucharist (the sacrament of holy Communion during the Mass) has a saving power.

However, the Lord Jesus clarified this controversial spiritual mystery: "The words that I speak unto you, they are spirit, and they are life" (John 6:63). The Bible teaches that "eating the flesh" of Christ means believing on him for eternal life, and his blood represents the Holy Spirit's baptism for salvation. Only true born-again believers are spiritually nourished with the joy of God's salvation (Psalm 51:12). Therefore, eating the flesh of Christ and drinking his blood simply refer to appropriating saving faith.

Growth

Have you ever seen a fifty-year-old man who is still crawling like a baby and living on milk? Of course not. Yet a fairly large number of believers are still acting like babies by not growing spiritually. The Bible calls them "carnal," meaning *fleshly* or *of the flesh*. Carnal Christians are unable to understand the deeper truths of God's Word, and they are characterized by Paul as being "babes in Christ. . . . There is among you envying, and strife, and divisions" (I Corinthians 3:1-3). All these problems emanate from spiritual immaturity. The Bible does not excuse ignorance, because the action of carnal Christians is scarcely distinguishable from that of unsaved men.

The reason for this ignorance is that carnal Christians are satisfied with their lukewarmness, and their shocking indifference to spiritual growth is accentuated by their apathy to God's Word. Furthermore, their carnal lifestyle gives "great occasion to the enemies of the Lord to blaspheme" (II Samuel 12:14; cf. Titus 2:5). On the other hand, spiritual growth requires a long period of gestation. The believer who studies the Bible diligently not only is showing himself "approved unto God," but also is rewarded for his obedience (II Timothy 2:15; Hebrews 11:6). Consequently, Christian maturity requires time to grow in the knowledge of the Word of God and to be able to discern between good and evil (Hebrews 5:12-14).

It is not only true that the blood of the human race has been poisoned by the deadly venom of Adam's sinful blood, but it is also true that the Lord and Savior Jesus Christ has the power to redeem us by his own sinless "blood out of every kindred, and tongue, and people, and nation" (Revelation 5:9). The Bible substantiates this truth in the following declaration: "For as in Adam all die, even so in Christ shall all be made alive" (I Corinthians 15:22).

In other words, since the blood of the human race is polluted with sin, the only way man can escape from being "tormented with fire and brimstone . . . for ever and ever: and . . . cast into the lake of fire" (Revelation 14:10, 11, 20:15) is to agree with God concerning man's total depravity, seek the Lord Jesus before it is forever too late, and call "upon him while he is near" (Isaiah 55:6). Therefore, since God the Savior is neither a Jew nor a Gentile, the unsaved person will do well to accept God's gracious invitation to salvation with no hesitation. For God promised, "If thou shalt confess with thy mouth the Lord Jesus, and shalt believe in thine heart that God hath raised him from the dead, thou shalt be saved" (Romans 10:9)!

Epilogue

I have struggled and agonized much for the last few years during the writing of this book. I have been discouraged and weakened by a barrage of Satanic obstructions. But in spite of these hindrances in the writing of this timely volume, the Lord Jesus kept stirring my heart and burdening my soul with thoughts of the neglected Arabs. Yes, Arabs are among the people yet to be evangelized. And to leave them unevangelized is to do nothing less than deprive more than one billion of the world's population of God's wonderful plan of salvation. For this reason, the Lord allowed me to experience in my dreams the "horror of great darkness" (Genesis 15:12), to underscore the severity of his wrath upon the unregenerate condition of my people, the Arabs. I wept bitterly on many occasions, and cried out to God to help me evangelize as many as possible, because "my heart's desire and prayer to God" is "that they might be saved" (Romans 10:1).

I sought the Lord for help and guidance, that I might find biblical and extra-biblical sources to substantiate the unique views presented in this study. He did not only lead me to the right sources for the little-known history and genealogy of Arabs (see Bibliography), but also gave me the necessary illumination to be able to clarify and expound upon several great controversial spiritual mysteries.

However, I am well aware that many biblical scholars and others will quickly find a reason to justify their subjective points of view concerning this controversial and provocative work. Some may even criticize the book and its author in a most unkind way. I am reminded of what happened to our dear Lord, and to Paul, who went through much more opposition. They were evangelizing and discipling their converts through sound doctrine. This is what I am trying to do, also.

Nevertheless, in the wake of recent and biblically predicted future world events, this book had to be written in order to stimulate the inquisitive reader toward more diligent biblical research, and to exhort believers to occupy themselves with evangelism rather than with political action. Hence, the point of this work is to emphasize the universality of God's love and to encourage Christians to fulfill the Great Commission, because "the time is at hand" (Revelation 1:3).

On the other hand, I am saddened by the mere fact that a multitude of books have been written on the prophetic implications of the Abrahamic Covenant in relation to the Promised Land and national Israel, while few were written on ways to evangelize Jews. Is the land and the nation of Israel more important than salvation? Consequently, by magnifying the land and its inhabitants, the writers were able to condition passive readers by inoculating them with false hopes concerning the salvation of Israel. God usually does not save an entire nation, but only redeemed individuals who abide "in the doctrine of Christ" (II John 9).

Finally, I would like to advise the reader who desires to obey the teachings of the Bible not to argue with God, but to agree with him, in that his sovereign purpose for Jews will not be fulfilled by their return to Palestine, but by their return to our Lord and Savior, Jesus Christ. Furthermore, God's sovereign purpose for Arabs and for others is the same. Therefore, instead of glorying in a particular land or nation, let us "glory in the Lord" (II Corinthians 10:17)!

Selected Bibliography

Albright, William Foxwell. *Archaeology and the Religion of Israel.* Baltimore: Johns Hopkins Press, 1942.

Berkhof, Louis. *The History of Christian Doctrines.* Grand Rapids: Baker Book House, 1976.

Davidson, A. B. *An Introductory Hebrew Grammar.* 24th ed. Revised by John Edgar McFadyen. New York: Charles Scribner's Sons, 1954.

De Haan, M. R. *The Chemistry of the Blood.* 8th ed. Grand Rapids: Zondervan Publishing House, 1943.

Gesenius, Wilhelm. *Hebrew Grammar.* Boston: I. Bradley and Co., 1850.

Hislop, Alexander. *The Two Babylons.* Neptune, N. J.: Loizeaux Brothers, 1959.

Hitti, Philip K. *History of the Arabs.* New York: St. Martin's Press, 1970.

————. *The Near East in History.* New York: D. Van Nostrand Co., 1960.

Ibn Khaldûn. *The Mugaddimah: An Introduction to History.* 3 vols. 2nd ed. Trans. Franz Rosenthal. Bollingen Series 43: Princeton University Press, 1967.

Ironside, Harry A. *Lectures on the Book of Revelation.* Neptune, N. J.: Loizeaux Brothers, 1973.

Jacob, B. *The First Book of the Bible, Genesis.* New York: KTAV Publishing House, 1934, 1974.

Josephus, Flavius. *Antiquities*. New York: Schocken Books, 1971.

Kittel, Rudolf, ed. *Biblica Hebraica*. Stuttgart: Wurttembergische Bibelanstalt, 1937.

Lightfoot, J. B. *The Apostolic Fathers*. Grand Rapids: Baker Book House, 1978.

Rushdoony, Rousas John. *The Foundations of Social Order*. Fairfax, Va.: Thoburn Press, 1978.

Schaeffer, Francis A. *Genesis in Space and Time*. Downers Grove, Ill.: Inter-Varsity Press, 1975.

Smith, William. *Dictionary of the Bible*. 4 vols. Cambridge: Riverside Press, H.O. Houghton & Co., 1868-70.

———. *The Old Testament History*. New York: Harper and Brothers, [© 1897].

Torrey, R. A. *Difficulties in the Bible*. Chicago: Moody Press, 1907.

Young, Robert. *Young's Analytical Concordance to the Bible*. New York: Funk & Wagnalls, 1936.

Author's Biographical Sketch

Louis Bahjat Hamada was born to an aristocratic Lebanese family, in the province of Houran (biblical Haran), a northeastern district of Syria, where his father was serving as prosecutor general under the French mandatory rule. It is interesting to note that Job was buried in that vicinity, and Abraham made his abode there before entering Canaan.

Dr. Hamada was raised in Lebanon after the untimely death of his parents. He was twelve years old when his grandfather, who ruled Lebanon as the religious head of the Druze sect, became his guardian. At the age of fifteen, he ran away from school to begin a career as a singer. In 1953 he came to America on a student scholarship and experienced a miraculous escape from a car accident, which culminated in his salvation on September 11, 1955. Since then, he has attained a reputation as soul-winner and Bible scholar. In addition, Dr. Hamada has earned a Ph.D. in music education from Florida State University and a Master's degree from Dallas Theological Seminary in Dallas, Texas. He is also an ordained minister.

Dr. Hamada is a noted international speaker and the executive director of a faith-ministry which takes him and his wife across America and abroad. Dr. Hamada has a unique and timely biblical view concerning world events as they relate to prophecy. While many are speculating on the date of the "Rapture," Dr. Hamada is feverishly seeking to impart a refreshing and sober approach to prophecy, on a balanced biblical interpretation, relating to Arabs and Jews in particular.

This book gives a penetrating analysis of the origin and heritage of Arabs and Jews, emphasizing "the ministry of reconciliation" in order that many may be reconciled to Jesus Christ (II Corinthians 5:18).

Dr. Hamada has ably traced the roots of Arabs and Jews to Shem; he expounds on Genesis 12:3, to determine the recipients of the blessings and curses mentioned there.

Dr. Hamada was officially inducted into the Oxford Society of Scholars on July 17, 1987. The selection of scholars is based on "excellence in research related to problem-solving within the family, community, and church and contributing to knowledge potentially enhancing the growth of Christianity." This affirmation was "attested by the Faculty of the Oxford Graduate School and the Board of Governors of the Oxford Society of Scholars."

The Hamadas are the only known Druze family with a full-time ministry. Dr. Hamada's faith is undergirded by a staunch, unswerving commitment to the inerrant, plenary inspiration and infallible written Word of God—THE BIBLE!

For speaking engagements, write:

Dr. Louis Hamada
P. O. Box 3333
Jackson, TN 38303